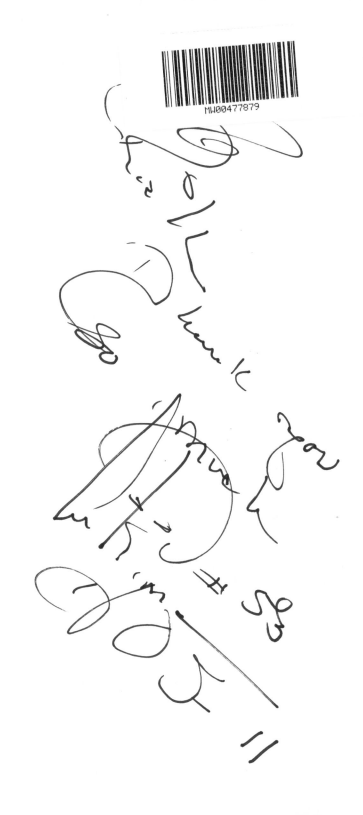

Here Comes the

A-Train!

Here Comes the

A-TRAIN!

The Story of Basketball Legend
ARTIS GILMORE

By **Artis Gilmore**

with **Mark Bruner** *and* **Reid Griffith Fontaine**

Acclaim Press
MORLEY, MISSOURI

Acclaim Press
— Your Next Great Book —

P.O. Box 238
Morley, MO 63767
(573) 472-9800
www.acclaimpress.com

Book & Cover Design: M. Frene Melton

ISBN: 978-1-942613-90-9 / 1-942613-90-3
Library of Congress Control Number: 2018901482

First Printing: 2018
Printed in the United States of America
10 9 8 7 6 5 4 3 2 1

This publication was produced using available information.
The publisher regrets it cannot assume responsibility for errors or omissions.

CONTENTS

Dedications

I have made my way in this world by having had the privilege of competing in a sport dominated by the strongest, most athletic, physically gifted men in the world.

I dedicate this book, however, to the strongest, most caring, lovingly gifted women in the world: my wife Enola Gay and my mother Mattie.

My mother's legacy to me includes a personality that is easy-going, slow to anger but willing and able to hold the high ground strongly when it's important to do so. My wife helped me shape those traits through her friendship and love and, to her, I owe much of what is good about the man I have become. Both women have been proud of my successes — both women have had my back when times got tough — both women have pushed me forward when I became discouraged or wanted to quit — both women will be my strength and my happiness, always.

I love them both.

Artis Gilmore

To my amazing, ever-loving, and dedicated mother, who still pushes me to pursue my potential, know my value, and succeed in all facets of life; and to whom I owe so much. I love you!

Reid Griffith Fontaine

ACKNOWLEDGMENTS

This is the most difficult part of preparing my memoirs.

There are, in fact, so many persons to whom I feel appreciation, respect, and love that naming each one individually would be a book in itself. I trust that those of you who are important to me know who you are and know how grateful I am for all you have done to support me and to make my life better with each passing year.

First and foremost, however, I must acknowledge the guiding force in my life, Jesus Christ.

Next: nothing is possible without the foundation of family — and, for me, that foundation is absolutely great. I truly hope that through my actions I can continue to thank my family for what they mean to me. Words fail me in my desire to express my endless love for my wife, Enola Gay, and our magnificent children: O.J., Priya, Shawna, Tifany, and Artis II.

So, too, am I forever appreciative of my professional family. I carry in my heart the many coaches, teammates, and opponents who were such a huge part of shaping my life. What we shared is exceptional and rare and rewarding. Special among those many wonderful persons: Joe Williams and Tom Wasdin, my former coaches. Also, in particular, I want to state, loud and clear, how privileged and proud I am to count among my dearest friends: Julius "Dr. J" Erving and George "The Iceman" Gervin. Thank you, thank you, thank you.

From a very personal perspective, I wish to thank Frank Pace, who has been an incredible friend since my collegiate years at Jacksonville. So too: Dr. Fran Kinne, my second "Mom," and Mr. W.W. "Bill" Gay, Sr., my former employer.

This book would not have been possible without the tenacity and commitment of Reid Fontaine and Andrew Tie, and I thank them for the fact that you are now reading these words.

Finally, but of equal importance, I want to say to all of the basketball fans who supported me through many years of both defeats and victories: I hope that by sharing my memories through this book I can repay you, in a small way, for making all of this possible. The roar of a full stadium is still in my ears. The energy of the crowd still makes my heart beat faster. The fact that you cared for me, cheered for me, and shared my life on the hardwood will warm me and gratify me forever.

Artis "A-Train" Gilmore
#53 H.O.F.

I am grateful to numerous individuals who have contributed either directly or indirectly to this project. First and foremost, I thank the book's editors. Andrew Tie played a very important role in this work. Andrew is a former sports writer and now higher education communications specialist, who brought excellent insight to the manuscript. He joined the project late in the process but truly helped to captain our ship to port. He also found us a perfect publisher in Acclaim Press. Speaking of Acclaim, enormous thanks go to their outstanding editorial team—Douglas Sikes, Randy Baumgardner, and Shirley Rash. Acclaim's passion, diligence, and intelligence were critical to the book's completion and are so very much appreciated. I also thank close friends who read iterations of this manuscript at varying points in its path: Kevin Becker, Taylor Sharp (who connected me with Andrew Tie), and Jim Taubenfeld, who is responsible for my introduction to Artis in Springfield, Massachusetts, in 2011, when Artis was being enshrined. In addition, I thank Jim's colleagues at the Naismith Memorial Basketball Hall of Fame, who have been so welcoming and supportive over the years, including John Doleva, Scott Zuffelato, and Sherman Brown. I would also like to thank Professor Kenneth A. Dodge, not only for his highly valued friendship over the years, but for the generous scholarly support he has provided me at and through Duke University. Finally, I find myself further indebted to my family for its unwavering support and, particularly, to my endlessly loving, understanding, and loyal mother, Constance J. Fontaine, a published author herself, to whom I dedicate this book.

Reid Griffith Fontaine

PREFACE

I had the tremendous pleasure of meeting the great Artis Gilmore in August 2011. Artis was about to be inducted into the Naismith Memorial Basketball Hall of Fame. A close friend and member of the Hall of Fame (HOF) Board of Governors, Jim Taubenfeld, invited me to the enshrinement ceremony and other HOF events. It was actually Jim's first time meeting the A-Train, as well.

We approached him to introduce ourselves at the Legends Brunch. Artis was very gracious but also looked like a deer in headlights. As I later learned, he simply felt overwhelmed with all of the attention, not to mention the anxiety a new inductee experiences in making sure all of his or her loved ones, friends, and other invited guests are taken care of and happy. Jim and I told Artis that we had always admired his career and talked with him for a few minutes about how the weekend was going for him.

When we parted, we shook hands. I make particular mention of this because it is well known that Artis does not know his own strength. I remember my bones grinding against each other as Artis shook my hand. Jim told me he had no feeling in his right hand. He then showed me a dark red mark at the base of his middle finger, made from a ring on his ring finger pressing into it as a result of his fingers being nearly crushed during their handshake. Artis is a powerful dude even to this day, long after his playing tenure.

At dinner that night, the Hall of Fame placed us at a table with some of Artis' family and close friends. So, with whom did I sit at that dinner? None other than Mark Bruner, Artis' long-time friend and web developer — not to mention co-author of this book. Small world. At that time, none of the three of us had any thought that we would work together on Artis' biography. Indeed, although I had met Artis earlier in the day and had a nice conversation with Mark and his son at that dinner, neither of them had much of an idea who I was … and certainly none of us could foresee the close relationship Artis and I would later develop.

At that point in time, Mark had long started work on this project. The initial intention was to write a book that highlighted Artis' importance to the game, largely so he would get more of the attention he deserved from the Hall of Fame. But the HOF already had its eye on Artis.

It had formed a special American Basketball Association (ABA) committee to identify key ABA players and figures who were deserving of enshrinement. When Artis was selected in 2011, he and his family were delighted. But other legendary players were befuddled. Why? They couldn't believe he wasn't already in the HOF! In fact, some members of the HOF even said that to him over the course of his enshrinement weekend: "Congrats, Train, but I have to admit, I thought you were inducted into the Hall years ago!"

Patience, as they say, is a virtue, which brings us to this book. In 2012, Artis first asked me to join this project, develop the manuscript, find a publisher, and be the closer. With the help of our editor, Andrew Tie, and publisher, Doug Sikes, here we are, at the end of a long and winding tunnel. We believe this book accurately captures Artis' greatness on the basketball court, his importance to both the ABA and NBA, and his ability to make all of the teams he played for better. But just as important is that we hope readers are able to glean the strength and goodness Artis has exhibited throughout his life as a man. He has demonstrated that you can be a forceful and dominant presence on the hardwood while still showing the caring and respect for others that human beings deserve. This, above all else, is what makes Artis one of the greats.

Reid Griffith Fontaine

INTRODUCTION

For many basketball fans of today's younger generation, Shaquille O'Neal, Kobe Bryant, and Tim Duncan are about as far back as the NBA goes. Memories of the good old days include Michael Jordan coming out of retirement (again!), Allen Iverson stepping over Tyronn Lue, and the emergence of a young man fresh out of high school by the name of LeBron James. Slightly older fans had the good fortune of witnessing M.J. in his prime. Before Jordan came Larry Legend and Magic, along with a decade of historic showdowns in the NBA Finals between the Celtics and Lakers. Keep going back through the record books and a bevy of first-name-only legends pop up: Kareem, Wilt, Oscar, and Doc. But Artis "A-Train" Gilmore? He's no household name. And he never was, not even in his prime. But the story that follows suggests he was right there with the best who ever laced it up.

Let's look at the facts: Artis averaged 22.7 rebounds per game at Jacksonville University, a mark that still stands the test of time as the highest average ever in Division I. He averaged more than 20 points and 20 rebounds in his two years in college. Let that sink in. Between his careers in the ABA and NBA, Artis won Rookie of the Year, earned an ABA Championship, made 11 All-Star games, and was enshrined in the Basketball Hall of Fame in 2011 as one of the game's best players in history. He also averaged close to 19 points and 12 rebounds in the pros. Until recently, he was the all-time NBA field-goal percentage leader and has only taken a back seat to dunking extraordinaire DeAndre Jordan. If you got the ball to the big man, he'd reward you with an assist. He was virtually unstoppable in the paint.

Why is Artis not remembered along with the very best of centers in basketball history? In basketball, it's all about the rings. So, while Artis led his Kentucky Colonels to an ABA Championship, along with other basketball greats like Dan Issel and Louie Dampier, he did not get a chip in the NBA. But part of the explanation is just as surely that a good portion of his career, and arguably much of his prime, was spent in the long-defunct American Basketball Association, the "little brother" league that sparkled with the flair and talent of other basketball legends like Rick Barry, Julius "Dr. J" Erving, George "The Iceman" Gervin, Moses Malone, and David "Skywalker" Thompson but never filled the shoes worn by the NBA. If all of his professional accolades were accrued in the NBA, history would look back differently on the A-Train. And, safe to say, he'd be a member of the NBA's 50 Greatest Players roster. His pensive approach and reserved personality may have something to do with how his basketball career is viewed historically, as well. Artis preferred to walk the walk, no talking required. A gentle giant? Maybe off the court, but good luck to you if you are between him and the orange iron.

Here Comes The A-Train! is a look into the life of Artis Gilmore, perhaps the best basketball player you've never heard of. He battled against many of those greats mentioned above, and he often came away victorious or with his head held high. Artis' career is full of tremendous accomplishments, but this book isn't merely a recanting of the good times. Artis takes a deep, introspective look at the trials in his own life, starting from the small, poor town of Chipley, Florida. He finds lessons in the hardships he faced, whether it is hunger in his youth or yearly playoff battles. He has never forgotten his roots and has always stayed true to himself throughout his career.

This book details Artis' biggest basketball moments — the NCAA Final against UCLA, the famous ABA dunk contest of 1976, learning under Coach Hubie Brown, etc. — which are, in and of themselves, enough to capture the attention and interest of casual and serious hoops fans alike. With the ABA having recently celebrated its 50th anniversary, it's a good time to look back on a league and a player that shaped basketball today. And the larger life lessons Artis reveals, such as taking strength from hardships and the search for finding balance in life, afford the reader an opportunity to walk away with some important and thoughtful reflections at the end of the ride.

Andrew Tie
Reid Griffith Fontaine

Here Comes the

A-TRAIN!

The Story of Basketball Legend
ARTIS GILMORE

One Night In Boston

PART ONE

The Great Ones Create

I remember when I saw my first live, professional basketball game like it was yesterday. It was December 22, 1967, at the most hallowed of basketball grounds: Boston Garden. No other court had more history, more mysteries, more personality. Under that floor, Boston Celtic trolls reportedly lived and haunted the dribbling of opposing players by conjuring up dead spots in the wood beneath their feet. It's as much a legend as the many players who started and ended their careers there or who merely passed through the cramped locker rooms, some on their way to greatness, others into mediocrity not recorded in basketball's history book.

I was 19 years old, a freshman at Gardner-Webb Junior College. I didn't grow up playing basketball on courts like the Boston Garden's. Until just a few years earlier, I knew basketball as a game played on outdoor courts of sand and gravel or, at best, cracked, uneven asphalt. Now, I was not only many miles away from my small hometown of Chipley, Florida, but I was also one pass of a basketball away from the fabled parquet floor.

Yes, Chipley was some 1,300 or so miles away, but even further in the world of basketball, where I had now reached the epicenter, surrounded by ghosts of Celtic dynasties past and by smoke from years of Red Auerbach's victory cigars. All this, of course, is the musing recollection of a man now long past his playing days. At the time, Ernie Fleming, my junior college basketball teammate and companion that night, and I were like any other young guys in the big city. Many things were on our minds, and basketball greatness probably wasn't high on the list.

Despite the fact that I stood 7 feet tall and had begun to attract interest from a variety of colleges and universities, the thought of basketball as a way of life had not evolved much in my mind. That night, however, I saw my first real glimpse of what greatness looks like. The Celtics, led by Bill Russell, faced the Cincinnati Royals and Oscar Robertson. As a kid, I revered Russell and Wilt Chamberlain.

I identified more with Chamberlain because of his titanic strength and warm, outgoing style, but anyone who has so much as casually experienced the game of basketball knew, and stood in awe of, the tremendous defensive and team-leading talents of Bill Russell.

On that night, however, it was Oscar Robertson who caught my attention. The "Big O" has often been referred to as basketball's first "big guard." Today's younger generation of fans wouldn't bat an eye seeing big men bringing the ball up court. Magic Johnson, at 6' 9", sticks out as the prototypical big guard in the minds of most fans under the age of 40. But Magic was only 8 years old in 1967, and Robertson, at 6' 5" and 220 pounds, was as big as a guard got in those days. He had an exceptionally strong upper body, and his legs could only be described as two machines made of muscle. To put his size in perspective, although Russell had about six inches on Robertson, the two men weighed approximately the same.

As the night progressed, I became more and more amazed by the way Oscar Robertson played the game. It was obvious that he had no fear in taking the ball and going directly at Russell. That was not showmanship. That was not a younger man acting out a macho fantasy by daring the best defender in pro basketball to stop him. Clearly, Robertson was a man who had a plan, and that plan was to create opportunities by sticking his head in the jaws of the lion. Each time he challenged Russell, he did it slightly differently. He would simultaneously jump and fling his body into Russell, hoping to draw a foul or create openings. He hip-checked. He grabbed wrists. He head-faked, shoulder-faked, ball-faked, performed every kind of fake-out move you could name. No move seemed without purpose. If it looked like he would turn left, he invariably turned right. When it appeared certain he would shoot, he would pass. When he seemed momentarily slow, he was only one step away from again turning on the gas. I suppose if I hunted through the record books, I could find out exactly how many points and assists Robertson made that night, but the numbers themselves don't really matter.

Despite Robertson's magic, though, it wasn't enough. Boston won the game 120-117 and later, in the playoffs, beat both Chamberlain's Philadelphia 76ers and Jerry West's Los Angeles Lakers to capture the NBA title in what was Bill Russell's penultimate season. To many people, the Celtics' victory would appear to be the only important measure from that night. After all, the object of sports is to win. What good is a great individual effort when the team loses? Yet as a teenager, I remember thinking and feeling something that I couldn't comprehend yet. I've come to realize it boils down to "The great ones create."

Looking back on that inspiring night, I had watched a number of greats: Bill Russell, John Havlicek, and Sam Jones for the Celtics and Oscar Robertson and Jerry Lucas for the Royals. But it was the ability to create, as showcased by Oscar Robertson, that gave me my first insights into what great men and women can do with a mastery of their talents.

But allow me a moment to extend this observation beyond basketball and into day-to-day life. It's unfortunately too easy to find people who simply wait for life to happen. Many of these folks remain unhappy their entire time on earth because of the static nature of their lives. Or worse: what happens is hurtful and destructive.

Truly great people are not immune to losses and tragedies. Sometimes the better team loses. Sometimes the events of life can't be controlled. These people are still humans, after all. Truly great people, however, do not wait for life to either happen or pass them by. They learn about themselves. They understand who they are, what motivates them, what drives them, what makes them happy. They create opportunities for greatness.

In doing so, they learn their strengths and are not afraid to take those strengths straight at the tallest, strongest obstacles in their paths, even if it's a 6-foot, 10-inch behemoth by the name of Bill Russell. They also come to know their weaknesses and spend as much energy as possible in reshaping or overcoming them. In the most hostile environments, against the best talent, and in the biggest moments, the "greats" not only get tougher and more determined, but they also learn who they are and play even better. The "greats," regardless of profession, transcend crucial and difficult moments and realize their ultimate potential, or true desires, no matter the outcome. That's what I learned from watching the "Big O" play in the Boston Garden.

Win, lose, or draw, the great ones create. In basketball, those acts of creativity are sometimes small and almost unnoticed. They are the unseen shifts of weight, movement of feet, peripheral vision, or the invisible drive of the heart wanting and willing to succeed. On the court, the great ones set solid picks for teammates to create driving lanes, the great ones dive on loose balls to create an extra possession, and the great ones box out to create rebounding opportunities. It's the same off the court, where true greatness does not mean tickertape parades or fame or money. It means small acts of kindness, genuine charity, and quiet love for all human beings.

⎯⎯∞⎯⎯

The NBA was in its 22nd season when I saw that thriller at the Garden between Russell and Robertson in December of 1967. That same year, another basketball league was born: the American Basketball Association. It was totally unimaginable to me back then, but the ABA would change my life.

One year earlier, the great Celtics player K.C. Jones had retired. Twenty-one years later, K.C. Jones would coach me in my final home game as an NBA basketball player. I would play that last game as a Boston Celtic. Where? Wouldn't you know ... on the storied parquet floor of Boston Garden.

BAREFOOT IN CHIPLEY

Politicians may wish that voters think they grew up Abraham Lincoln-style, in a log cabin, educating themselves by reading books by the light of wood fires. The basketball version of the "when I was young" story features the hoopster as a child, nailing up an old peach basket and shooting a rolled-up ball of old socks until well after dark, through blazing hot weather, rain, and cold. The difference between these myth-building descriptions of childhood is that, for many basketball players, the stories are actually true. Over the years, writers have described me as reticent and shy. I mention this now because it has an influence on my attitudes about sharing details of my life — and that, obviously, is what a memoir is all about.

I suppose shy people never think of themselves as shy. Maybe I am, but if so, it's never been an impediment to having a wonderful and growing circle of friends who have been a lifelong source of enjoyment and support. As to being quiet, I guess I am. According to my biography on the NBA website, I "barely spoke above a whisper." I like a good conversation with friends, and I really don't have many reservations about visiting with people I've never met before. However, I do have problems talking about what I have achieved on the basketball court. In some ways, it's easier for me to talk about the losses than it is to describe the victories. I always saw it as boastful to highlight the big wins. After all, the losses are as much a part of my basketball record as the wins are. In a similar way, I am uncomfortable describing my early days as a basketball player.

Some of my earliest games sound like they were invented by a public relations agency. We didn't always have an actual basketball and often played with a smooth rubber ball not much larger than a grapefruit. When we didn't have a ball, we used empty tin cans, and those didn't dribble too well. Our hoop was an old bicycle rim tacked up to the outside of a building.

But guess what? I'm only one of thousands of ballplayers whose first years began in very much the same way, shooting with tennis balls, bundles of rubber band-wrapped rags, or anything that resembled a ball, and shooting at tin pails, holes in the wall, or anything that resembled a hoop. I don't want to pretend to be special in that way. It's just the way it was.

I was born on September 21, 1948, and grew up in a very small town, Chipley, in the northwest panhandle of Florida. There were not many opportunities for young folks. Typically, at the beginning of each school year, there would be about 30 kids in the graduating class. At the end of the year, less than half would actually graduate. The rest had left to help their families work the fields or raise unexpected families of their own. Even today, more than a fifth of Chipley's population of approximately 3,600 remain below the poverty line. They do have indoor basketball, though — something that did not exist when I was a kid because there was no gym. Our courts ranged from one that was paved with tar to others that were not much more than sand, gravel, and holes.

Read the biographies of many other ABA and NBA basketball players, and you'll find a large roster of guys whose childhood surroundings were not exactly long on real opportunities. Whether it is the inner city ghetto or the small rural farm, young ballplayers have a long history of rising above their environments because of their passion for the game. One of my favorite quotes about growing up in a small town comes from the great New York Knick, Willis Reed, who described his birthplace of Hico, Louisiana, to *Pro Basketball Illustrated* as "so tiny that it didn't even have a population." Today, of course, with the globalization of basketball, growing up in hard surroundings goes beyond the borders of the United States and includes dedicated young ballplayers from all over the planet.

I suppose it's fair to say that I grew up in extreme poverty conditions. It has been written that my father was a fisherman, making it sound like that is what he did for a living. But we didn't view it that way. When he fished, it was often because that was the only way we would have anything to eat, so his fishing was less of a vocation and more of a necessity. When I say "we," I mean six boys, two girls, plus my mother, Mattie, and my father, Otis. That is 10 hungry mouths to feed.

I slept in the same bed of our three-room, tar-papered, kerosene-lit shack house with two of my brothers until I was 16. At Christmas, we would get the Sears Roebuck catalog, which we kids called "The Pretend Book." We made believe we would get anything we wanted from the catalog. Of course, we never got anything because my parents couldn't afford gifts. Sometimes at Christmas we didn't even have food unless neighbors brought a fruit basket.

Obviously, those were days long before $200 basketball shoes became a necessity for any well-dressed young ballplayer. I was a tall string bean, and by the time I was 12 years old, I wore a size 12 shoe. At 13, I wore a size 13 shoe. Or, to be more accurate, I would have worn a size 12 or 13, except that my family couldn't afford that large of a shoe for either basketball or normal wear. For several years as an early teen, I simply went barefoot. That was not only a daily challenge but also a real problem as I grew more and more involved with organized sports. I wore a hodgepodge of shoes while playing ball — ranging from loafers to wingtips. My feet were constantly blowing out of the sides of those shoes as if they were bad tires. One time, I actually found a pair of low-cut sneakers that, to my amazement, were too large for me. I gave them up after a few minutes of playing time because I kept running out of them. Barefoot again!

But I'm no different from all the other basketball players who grew up in poverty. In fact, in my era and the generation before me, many young guys turned to basketball because it was the "poor kids" sport. Basketball in those days didn't have the historic All-American mystique of baseball, and it was cheap. You could play all day without paying a cent.

I recall the great Celtic guard Jo Jo White saying that, as a kid in St. Louis, he spent so much time playing basketball away from home that his father assumed that his son had fallen in with a bad crowd and was probably off doing drugs and committing crimes. Jo Jo had to prove himself by taking his dad to watch him play in a game.

Basketball history is filled with stories of men who have overcome the hardships of youth. Isiah Thomas grew up in one of the poorest, most dangerous neighborhoods in West Chicago, sleeping on the floor, going without heat and food, becoming the head of his family; his father left when Isiah was 3 years old. More recently, Allen Iverson also grew up in the worst of neighborhoods in Virginia, supporting his family after his father figure was incarcerated and bills piled up due in part to the poor health of a younger sister. During my playing days, so many guys came up the hard way that Detroit Pistons center Bill Laimbeer, whose father was a highly successful businessman, once joked that he was the only NBA player whose dad actually made more money than he did.

Jumping back for a moment to the subject of keeping basketball players from playing barefoot, a study has shown that NBA centers, on average, wear out 40-45 pairs of basketball shoes per season. Forwards tear through 35-40 pairs. Guards, probably because they don't work as hard as us big guys, burn out only about 30 pairs a year!

Shoes or no shoes, I can't say that I'd wish my childhood on anyone else, but at the same time, much of what I like about myself today, and three of the best lessons I learned, came from those early days.

First lesson: Don't feel sorry for yourself.

It slows you down and, besides, there are always people worse off. I traveled with a large group of current and former NBA players as part of Habitat for Humanity's Hurricane Katrina relief effort in New Orleans. I will never forget the images and scenes I witnessed. I'm still shocked to have seen a large portion of a major American city living like a Third World country without clean water or reliable electricity, months after the storm occurred. Sometimes the war against poverty is made out to be a part of the distant past, but sadly, that is not true.

Feeling sorry or not feeling sorry for oneself is purely a matter of personal motivation. Just think of how many professional athletes you have heard singing the blues because a new contract was for $55 million rather than $56 million. In 2004, Latrell Sprewell of the Minnesota Timberwolves, during contract extension negotiations, complained that he might hold out for more money because "I got my family to feed." He was due to make $14.6 million that year. Enough said.

Even odder, how about celebrities complaining that they have *too* much fame and fortune, and now they can't handle their success or enjoy their privacy? It seems to me that if you seek public attention, you can't just expect to tell the public to go away when you want a moment to yourself!

Those of us who follow basketball are well aware of the fact that a growing number of young players apparently feel that referees are out to get them. When a call does not go a player's way, he will complain, he will pout, but most disturbingly, he often won't even hustle down court to help his teammates. Many points have been scored while a "poor me" player has stopped to futilely argue his case with a ref or is sulking down court with a slow burn, just to let the fans know he has been wronged.

When I played, I rarely argued with referees. Of course I didn't always agree with the calls, but I'd never seen a successful argument made, so it wasn't worth my time. Plus, it's a simple fact that refs, as human beings, remember the guys who cause them the most aggravation. You can't tell me that there aren't paybacks somewhere along the line. I once saw the slogan: "Don't complain — organize." That makes a lot of sense to me. The time a person spends complaining about life is time taken away from organizing a better life.

Having said all that, there are people who can't make their lives better because they are sick, oppressed, or otherwise limited in what they can do. This is more reason, then, for the rest of us to organize our lives to help not only ourselves but also others who truly need us. The same holds true, on a much smaller scale, in the world of sports. Maybe the young guy who is complaining because he often gets called for traveling violations should stop griping and organize himself to better his fundamentals and improve his dribbling and footwork.

Second lesson: Some of the best things in life are accidental, unexpected, and unplanned.

Think of the many times in your life when unexpected events, sights, sounds, tastes, and people became truly great experiences. My life in basketball had its accidental qualities, too. I didn't plan to be 7' 2". My mom was only about 6' 2" and my dad was just 5' 8", so my height wasn't exactly predictable. I didn't plan to have athletic gifts or physical strength. In fact, I didn't even start playing basketball because I was interested in the game myself — my older brother George is responsible for that. He was my one older sibling, so I looked up to him, as he was my protector, provider, and role model in a lot of ways. Ironically, he motivated me to get involved, but he actually wasn't all that dedicated to sports. He played a little football and possessed good speed, but he had plenty of other interests. Lots of guys looked up to George, and he always found plenty of mischievous things to get involved in other than sports. I've come to suspect that George liked the fact that sports for teenagers is, in part, a popularity contest that gives a young man certain access to the young ladies. That may have been his objective, but it put me on a path for life that I certainly never planned.

I guess because of my size, the game took to me right away. I enjoyed basketball not because I played well but rather because playing ball helped me to focus on something other than the environment at home, which was at times very difficult. My mother and father fought all the time. I mean they literally physically fought each other. They could have very easily injured each other … or worse — taken a life. I am not exaggerating this. But we were lucky that didn't happen.

My father was born in 1900 and grew up around Chipley. He came from a family of nine brothers and four sisters. He received no schooling except for the well-known school of hard knocks. He was also very old school in other ways. My father's name was Otis, but everyone around town knew him as Pops or Poppa Stoppa. When I was real young, I didn't know what his real name was, and I was afraid to ask. That should tell you something. My mother wanted to name me Jerome but a neighbor suggested the name Artis. My mother liked this idea and asked how it was spelled. Artis was close to Otis, but not too close, so Artis it was.

There was very little employment available for him, and he worked various odd jobs to make ends meet. As a result, I was not the first Gilmore in my family to play professional sports. Poppa Stoppa's nickname grew out of his skill as a pool player. For him, pool was a way of supporting the family and also gaining respect. Even late in life, he remained a real gunslinger in the pool room, and young guys would stop in town looking to knock Poppa Stoppa off in a game. It was a big deal.

My father was about 24 or 25 years older than my mother, Mattie, and was 49 years old when I was born. There were other noticeable differences between my parents as well. My mother was more than 6 feet tall, but Poppa Stoppa could only muster 5' 8" if he was jumping up and down. My mother grew up in a real small town, Noma, not far from Chipley. She had a second or third grade education. Occasionally, she would find some employment, but she had a house full of young kids, so there was very little time for her to do anything but take care of us. My father had been married several times before and had other children, but in our Chipley house, there were, in order of age, George, me, Earl, Patrick, Thomas, Diane, Ossie, and Oren.

I realize now that except for one other family, we were the poorest in Chipley. I don't state this for sympathy but to point out how circumstances beyond one's control sometimes work for the best. In my case, growing up without money caused me to always remind myself that money is only as good as the person who uses it for good. When I signed my first big contract, I experienced the joy of being able to buy my mother a better house, get her teeth fixed, and get Poppa Stoppa the truck he wanted. As you might imagine, they were overjoyed and very proud.

As a young man with money in my pocket for the first time, I naturally spent some on myself. I liked having new cars. I couldn't resist a maroon Rolls Royce or a fur-lined Chevy van. I also bought a full-length beaver fur coat, which I showcased in a 1987 issue of *People* magazine. I also had a red jumpsuit or two in the wardrobe at that time, but those are images better off forgotten in my later years! Despite such luxuries, my childhood taught me the value of a dollar without making me a stingy or selfish person. If this assessment of myself is correct, then the tough times had their benefit. In his book: *Drive: The Story of My Life*, Larry Bird tells the story about me needing a new set of tires for my car. When I went to pick the car up from the garage, the owner said I could have the tires for free because I was Artis Gilmore. I refused the gesture and insisted he take the money because, as I told him, "If I were a poor man, he would make me pay." It wasn't right for me to take something for nothing just because I was a pro athlete. I'm not repeating the story to make myself seem like a saint — I'm certainly not one — it's just that I tried to do what I believed to be right.

Third lesson: You don't need riches to know what enriches life.

My parents didn't have a lot, materially speaking, but they taught me so much. I was well into my late teens before my father learned to write his own name. His childhood had been even poorer than mine. School was just not part of the equation for him, yet he was very serious about my need to get an education. He may not have been able to provide many material goods, but my father's legacy to me was a life-long appreciation for the need to always be learning, to always be growing, and to actively support others who seek to do the same.

My mother's legacy to me was similar but also included personality traits that were common to both of us. She wasn't quick to anger, nor am I. Yet she could only be pushed so far, after which she would get her back up and hold her ground. I like to think that she instilled that quality in me as well.

To give you an example: once when I was a child, my siblings and I were hungry, as usual, and we stole a watermelon from a farmer's field. The farmer saw us, and a policeman soon showed up at our house and began yelling at us. We were completely terrified and intimidated. My mother came out of the house and asked what the problem was, but the policeman was very rude. It wasn't that she was trying to excuse our actions, but she wanted to understand the situation and protect us the best she could. The policeman refused to address her questions and, in fact, told her that if she did not go back in the house, he would arrest her. Mother said something in return, the policeman grabbed her, and they went at it right there on the porch.

During the fight, my mother knocked the policeman over a stove that sat on the porch, knocking off the pipe, sending ashes and soot all over. When he got the upper hand, the policeman handcuffed my mother and took her to the station. Everyone there knew she had a house full of kids to take care of, so they sent her home soon and the whole incident blew over. The fact of the matter was, however, that in those days a black woman fighting with a policeman could very easily have been killed and nothing would have been done about it. My mother knew this but, right or wrong, no one was going to mess with her kids. She was a combination of gentleness and toughness, and that, to me, is a legacy to be proud of.

Both my parents were happy for my accomplishments on the basketball court, but I always believed that they would have felt the same toward me regardless of what I did as long as I was a moral, decent, educated man. My father was able to see me play on a number of occasions, especially later in my NBA career. It was more difficult for my mother, though. For years she had the family to tend to. Then diabetes attacked her health and sapped her energy, leading to her becoming a double amputee for the last 10 years of her life. I do have a favorite story, however, about the one and only game my mother watched me play at Jacksonville University.

In my first year at JU, we played a nationally relevant game against Florida State, coached by the great Hugh Durham and led by future Hall-of-Fame big man Dave Cowens. We traveled to Tallahassee, just 85 or so miles from Chipley. We played poorly and lost 89-83, our only regular-season loss of the 1969-70 season. Although we got our revenge by later beating Florida State on our home floor 85-81, I could never convince my mother that it wasn't her fault we lost. I've heard of superstitious athletes — but I had a superstitious mother who somehow thought that her presence had jinxed the Jacksonville Dolphins!

It surprises some people that basketball was not my first love, but rather it was football that first entranced me. In Chipley that's all you saw on television, and everyone wanted to play football, including me. I played football for a bit, but as a skinny 6' 5" freshman in high school, I suffered a minor injury. My parents couldn't afford the insurance premium required for me to play high school football, so that was the end of that.

As I said earlier, my life in basketball started in a way that wasn't very dramatic. It wasn't because I was big or strong or athletically gifted. It was because my older brother pushed me into it.

Basketball and I started our relationship when I was probably in fourth or fifth grade. Our teams would play the other elementary schools in the area. During that time, racial issues were very strong, and it was a difficult period throughout the South. Because this was before integration, all our games were against other segregated black grade schools. Road trips were especially tough. There was often little or no food at home when I returned from a game. On some occasions our road trips were as far as 90 miles away — a long haul for young kids. We rarely had money to stop on the side of the road to eat, and even if we did, it was a different era. Stopping at a store late in the evening for black kids was not a safe option.

The first coach who really saw my potential and capability was my elementary school coach, Albert Robertson. It's interesting how, in sports and life, even a few brief moments with someone who cares enough to share his time can help determine a true direction. Mr. Robertson was important because I was learning, he was there, and he cared.

We had to practice and play outdoors, and I finally got to practice in an indoor gym in junior high school.

I continued to play and I continued to grow, both vertically and in skill. By the age of 14, I was about 6' 4" and joined the basketball team at Roulhac High School, where we actually played in an indoor gym. From Roulhac, I went to Chipley High School, though my stay was very brief. After only a week or so, it was immediately clear to me that there was considerable racial tension at Chipley, which was predominately white. For this reason, I thought moving 35 miles away to all-black Carver High School in Dothan, Alabama, was a smarter choice for my senior year.

Carver High School in Dothan was considerably larger. Moving there was probably the single biggest step in my early growth as a basketball player. As a senior, I had a breakout year, including one 75-point game, and was honored as a third-team high school All-American behind Howard Porter and Jim Mc-Daniels. It was also at this time in my life that I got my first glimpse outside my childhood world and began to feel an inkling of where basketball could take me. I had shoes that fit. I had food to eat. I stayed with a family as a boarder — but I had my own bed for the first time ever!

The summer after my senior year, I was thrilled to receive an invitation to Camp Green Lane run by Villanova coach Jack Kraft. This was one of the nation's top high school basketball camps, and players could attend for free by working as waiters. All of the games and drills were played on outdoor courts. Chet Walker and Wali Jones of the Philadelphia 76ers came over to Camp Green Lane that summer, and that was a really big deal for us. Word was going around that Wilt Chamberlain might also make an appearance. Unfortunately, that never happened, but just the thought of Chamberlain dropping by had the camp abuzz. I remember looking forward to the chance of meeting him and being so excited about it because I had been such a huge fan of him and Bill Russell for so many years. I think a lot of it had to do with the fact that they both played center, and I was a young big man who aspired to play like them. Also in those early years, the only NBA regular season games that you would regularly see on television were those played between the Boston Celtics and the Philadelphia 76ers.

By then, I had shot up to 6' 9" and was feeling pretty good about my opportunities as a basketball player. However, one big obstacle got in my way: grades. Bad ones. I was unable to make the move to a Division I university. As a result, I made a two-year stop at Gardner-Webb Junior College in Boiling Springs, North Carolina.

Those years were important because they were the first stretches of time in my life spent away from family. I began to learn to live as an independent man. It wasn't always easy. I was homesick often. Once I called my mother to say that I wanted to quit and come home. Her reply: "Sure — come on home, you have such a great future in Chipley!" I saw her point and stayed at Gardner-Webb, which turned out to be a good decision.

My game improved under the guidance of knowledgeable coaching. This was also the first integrated team I ever played on. Of greater importance, my sense of personal responsibility grew. I began to overcome the natural fear of the different and unknown and started to realize that having and working toward goals can help defeat fear, racism, poverty, and loneliness. I met my future wife, Enola Gay. I worked at managing my time better, and this paid off in a big way in the classroom. I added weight and strength (although I was now more than 7 feet tall, I barely topped 200 pounds). My low post game improved. By the end of my sophomore year, I was ready for primetime collegiate basketball. Despite offers from many colleges, I surprised many people by choosing a scholarship from a school almost unknown to the basketball world: Jacksonville University.

I can give you many reasons why I chose Jacksonville, but the biggest of all was that I was comfortable there, and it was close to home. I may have grown during my two years at Gardner-Webb — both emotionally and to the height of 7' 2" — but I was still a country kid from Chipley, Florida, at heart. Even though Chipley was a 10-hour drive back then, it still felt much closer to home.

Jacksonville is where I went. Indeed, it's where I live to this day.

Artis as a young boy, 7 or 8 years old.

Elementary School

This Certifies That

Artis Gilmore

having satisfactorily completed the Course of Study prescribed
for the Elementary Department is entitled to Promotion into the

High School Department

May 31, 1960
Date of Award

Roulhac High School
School

Chipley, Florida
Town

J. L. McNeill
Principal

Superintendent

Artis Gilmore's mother, Mattie L. Gilmore.

Artis' dad, Otis Gilmore.

Artis Gilmore, graduation photo from high school, 1967.

Artis Gilmore student photo, Gardner-Webb Junior College, 1967-68.

Ernie Fleming and Artis Gilmore signing with Gardner-Webb Junior College with Coach Eddie Holbrook, 1967-68.

Artis at Gardner-Webb Junior College, 1967-68

Artis at Gardner-Webb Junior College with a college booster's son, 1967-68.

Artis goes up for a shot playing for Gardner-Webb Junior College, 1967-68.

HERE COME THE BULLDOGS . . .

1968-69 GARDNER-WEBB COLLEGE BASKETBALL SCHEDULE

Nov.	21	Friendship Jr. College	Home	17-18	G-W & Mercer (DBHDR)	Home
	23	Wingate	There	21	Spartanburg	There
	26	Spartanburg	Home	23	Wingate	Home
	30	Warren Wilson	Home	25	Brevard	There
Dec.	5	Wake Forest	Home	27	Kings	There
	7	Clemson	There	30	Lees-McRae	Home
	12	Anderson	Home	Feb. 4	Gaston	There
	14	U. N. C.	Home	7	Anderson	There
	20-21	G-W Holiday Tournament	Home	11	Lees-McRae	There
Jan.	4	Indian River, Fort Pierce, Fla.	There	13	Kings	Home
	6	Miami Dade, Miami Fla.	There	15	North Greenville	Home
	8	Abraham Baldwin, Tifton, Ga.	There	17	Gainesville	Home
	11	Clemson	Home	20	Brevard	Home
	14	North Greenville	There	22	Wake Forest	There

27-28-Mar. 1 Conference Tournament Forest City

Colors - Red & White

Coach: Eddie Holbrook

Assistants: Ron Hooper

Ken Daves

Gardner-Webb Junior College, 1968-69, team practice and schedule.

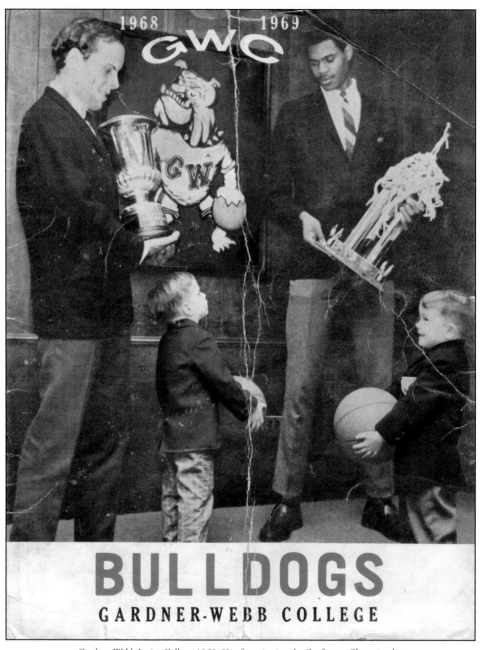

Gardner-Webb Junior College, 1968-69, after winning the Conference Championship.

*Artis Gilmore at
Jacksonville University.*

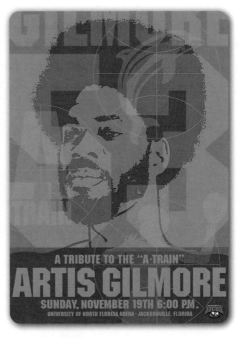

Artis with wife, Enola Gay Gilmore, when Artis was awarded his honorary doctorate at Jacksonville University.

Artis Gilmore at Jacksonville University.

Mike Storen introduces Frank Ramsey as Colonels head coach, 1970-71.

Artis Gilmore (middle left), Julius Erving (middle right), and Bobby Jones (right) at a basketball camp.

Artis Gilmore with Bobby Jones.

This picture was taken the day Artis signed with the Kentucky Colonels and was introduced at a Colonels' game.

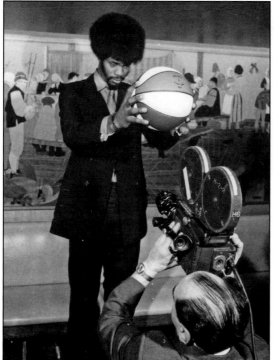

The day after Artis Gilmore signed with the Kentucky Colonels he appeared at a press conference at Toots Shor's Restaurant in New York City, March 17, 1971.

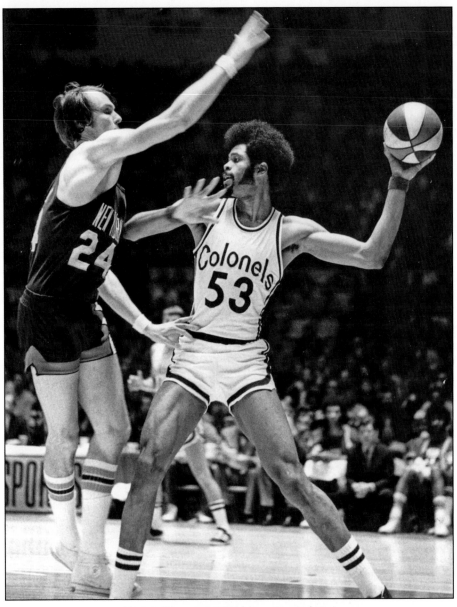

#53 Artis Gilmore and #24 Rick Barry (New York Nets).

*Artis Gilmore shooting over
Kareem Abdul-Jabbar.*

*#53 Artis Gilmore and
#33 Kareem Abdul-Jabbar
(Milwaukee Bucks).*

ABA vs. NBA: Colonels vs. Baltimore Bullets pre-season game. Rookie #54 Artis Gilmore faces Baltimore Bullets #41 Wes Unseld. Looking on are #12 John Tresvant and #3 Fred Carter. September 22, 1971. Photo by Mark Gordon.

Artis goes high to block a shot by the Virginia Squires #35 Willie Sojourner. Also pictured are #24 Neil Johnson, Mike Pratt, and Walt Simon. October 27, 1971. Photo by Mark Gordon.

Artis was interviewed by the voice of the Colonels, Van Vance. October 30, 1971. Photo by Mark Gordon.

Artis with Pierre Russell, Kentucky Colonels, 1971-72 ABA Season.

That big left hook by the Big A. #35 Roger Brown, #10 Rick Mount, and #35 Darel Carrier. November 13, 1971. Photo by Mark Gordon.

Always a battle against the Indiana Pacers... "Not this time Rick". #10 Rick Mount, #34 Mel Daniels, #30 George McGinnis, #9 Cincy Powell, and #32 Mike Gale. November 13, 1971. Photo by Mark Gordon.

1971-72 ABA East All-Star Team, front row, left to right: Charlie Scott, Warren Jabali, George Thompson, Louie Dampier, Mack Calvin, and Bill Melchionni. Back row: Coach Joe Mullaney, John Brisker, Jim McDaniels, Artis Gilmore, Dan Issel, Julius Erving, Rick Barry, and trainer Lloyd Gardner.

Artis Gilmore is presented the award for being named the 1971-72 ABA Most Valuable Player. Making the presentation is Jim O'Brien, sportswriter for Basketball Times and The Sporting News. April 4, 1972. Photo by Mark Gordon.

Artis slams home two of his 14 points as #44 Denver Rockets Ralph Simpson knows not to contest. ABA East All-Stars defeated the West, 142-118. January 29, 1972. Photo by Mark Gordon.

The Pacers' #25 Gus Johnson tries to defend #53 Artis Gilmore. Artis won the battle by scoring a game-high 29 points and grabbing 26 rebounds. April 30, 1973. Photo by Mark Gordon.

OFFICIAL ABA BOX SCORE:

Kentucky Colonels vs **New York Nets** DATE 2-3-74

SITE Nassau Coliseum OFFICIALS Walt Rooney, Jack Madden ATT 14,516

No.	Kentucky Colonels	Pos	Min	2-Pt M	2-Pt A	3-Pt M	3-Pt A	FT M	FT A	Reb Off	Reb Def	Reb Tot	Assists	Errors	Fouls	Total Points
25	Jim Bradley	F	22	3	5	0	0	2	2	1	7	8	1	4	2	8
44	Dan Issel	F	38	9	22	0	0	8	9	4	5	9	0	3	1	26
53	Artis Gilmore	C	42	9	15	0	0	3	5	6	34	40	9	7	2	21
10	Lou Dampier	G	29	6	11	0	0	0	0	0	0	0	5	1	2	12
11	John Roche	G	28	9	14	0	1	8	8	1	1		2	4	5	26
2	Walt Simon	F	11	2	5	0	0	0	0	0	1		1	4	2	4
3	Joe Hamilton	G	20	3	6	2	2	0	0	2	1		1	3	0	12
8	Ron Thomas	F	14	3	6	0	0	0	0	1	6	7	0	0	2	6
9	Red Robbins	F	13	1	8	0	0	0	0	3	1	4	0	1	0	2
15	Chuck Williams	G	19	1	2	0	0	0	0	0	1		5	3	0	2
22	Collis Jones	F	4	1	2	0	0	2	3	0	1		0	0	1	4
	TOTALS		240	47	96	2	3	23	27	18	58	76	24	30	17	123

PERCENTAGES .490 .667 .852 TEAM REBS. DEAD BALLS 2
TOTAL FG PCT .495 TOT. REBS. 8

No.	New York Nets	Pos	Min	2-Pt M	2-Pt A	3-Pt M	3-Pt A	FT M	FT A	Reb Off	Reb Def	Reb Tot	Assists	Errors	Fouls	Total Points
32	Julius Erving	F	35	7	20	2	2	1	1	4	3	7	5	3	2	21
35	Larry Kenon	F	30	7	17	0	0	0	1	5	7	12	0	1	1	14
40	Willie Sojourner	C	18	2	12	0	0	0	0	2	5	7	1	0	5	4
12	Mike Gale	G	34	2	10	0	1	2	2	4	4	8	6	0	4	6
23	John Williamson	G	30	9	22	0	0	2	3	4	1	5	1	3	3	20
4	Wendell Ladner	F	32	2	8	2	7	0	0	1	4	5	3	2	6	10
5	Billy Paultz	C	18	4	10	0	0	0	2	2	2	4	1	1	2	8
15	Billy Schaeffer	F	15	1	4	0	1	0	0	2	2	4	0	1	0	2
25	Bill Melchionni	G	23	1	7	0	3	0	0	1	2	3	4	2	2	2
44	Jim O'Brien	F	5	1	3	0	0	2	3	1	0	1	0	2	0	4
	TOTALS		240	36	113	4	14	7	12	26	30	56	21	15	25	91

PERCENTAGES .319 .286 .583 TEAM REBS. DEAD BALLS 2
TOTAL FG PCT .323 TOT. REBS. 6

BLOCKED SHOTS

Roche	1	Erving	3
Bradley	1	Ladner	1
Issel	1	Gale	
Gilmore	7	Schaeffer	1
Hamilton	1		

Goal Tending: Schaeffer - 1

STEALS

Issel		Gale	4
Williams		Williamson	3
Bradley		Paultz	1
Simon	1	Ladner	2
Robbins	1	Schaeffer	1
Jones	1	Kenon	1
		Melchionni	
		Sojourner	

	1	2	3	4		Total
Kentucky	25	34	33	31		123
New York	25	20	27	19		91

TECHNICAL FOULS:

REMARKS: Artis Gilmore's 40 rebounds is new ABA record, breaking George McGinnis record.

Stats sheet showing Artis Gilmore's incredible performance of 40 rebounds in one game.

CLUB REGULATIONS AND FINES - IF VIOLATED

RULE	FINE

1. Each player must take <u>notebook</u> on all road trips – during exhibition play. Team meetings will be held during this time period. — $ 50.00
   Replacement for lost notebook. — $ 250.00

2. If a player misses a scheduled flight departure, charter or commercial – Be at airport at least one-half hour before departure. — Player will pay his own transportation expenses.

3. On all road trips, players will dress neatly – Also be neatly dressed around hotel lobbies. — $ 50.00

4. On road trips – (a) Night before a game – curfew at 12:30; (b) If no scheduled game the following night, curfew is 2:00 a.m. — 1st Offense – $ 250.00
   2nd Offense – Double

5. A) Bus departures, hotel departures, practice times. — $ 5.00 for each late minute starting at 6th minute

   B) Reporting on time in locker room for <u>all</u> games –
      1. All players will be in locker room 1 HOUR and 15 MINUTES before game time. — First 15 Min. $ 50.00 / 15-30 Min. – $ 100.00 / 30-60 Min. – $ 150.00
      2. All players will be dressed, taped, etc. 50 minutes before each game for pre-game meeting in seats. — $ 50.00

   C) Missed practice – unless permission granted by Coach. — $ 250.00

   D) Missed game – unless permission granted by Coach. — $ 500.00

6. No smoking in game or practice arenas. — $ 50.00

7. No drinking will be allowed in hotel bars where we stay on all road trips, exhibition and regular schedule, or on any commercial flights. — 1st Offense – $ 250.00 / 2nd Offense – $ 500.00

8. Issued equipment bags must be used for all games. No laundry bags or pillow cases. — $ 50.00

9. Appointments must be kept with trainer at designated time, for treatment of all injuries. — 1st Offense – $ 50.00 / 2nd Offense – Double

10. No fraternizing with opponents prior to any league game. Following the game it is perfectly okay. The night of a game, let's get our minds on winning. This is your "Bread and Butter." — 1st Offense – $ 50.00 / 2nd Offense – Double

11. No player is allowed to leave practice gym without permission from Head Coach. — $ 50.00

CLUB REGULATIONS, cont.

RULE	FINE

12. At all practices - whether at home or on the road – all players will dress at practice site, unless instructed otherwise by the Coach. — $ 50.00

13. Girls in room on game day (EXPLAIN). — $ 250.00

14. Card Playing - no money showing at any time on commercial flights. — $ 250.00

15. Missing uniform at game time causing a player to forfeit playing time. — $ 250.00

We hope that no fines have to be imposed during the entire season. If each player is doing his job, this will be accomplished. We do not fine anyone, you fine yourself for lack of responsibility as a professional athlete. Let's discipline ourselves as men for respect of our teammates and the fine profession we represent as professional athletes.

In Coach Hubie Brown's 1974-75 playbook, page 1 was a letter stating the expectations of the team. Page 2 was the Club Regulations and Fines.

On November 9, 1974, Muhammad Ali attended our game against the New York Nets and Dr. J. On October 30, Ali and George Foreman crossed the ropes in a bout for the rights to claim the title of World Heavyweight Champion. The fight was held in Kinshasa, Zaire, Africa. With 12 seconds remaining in the eighth round, Foreman stumbled to the canvas. As referee Zack Clayton got to the eight count, Foreman could not get up. Photo by Mark Gordon.

Artis pulls down another rebound against Marvin Barnes and Maurice Lucas of the Spirits of St. Louis. February 19, 1975. Photo by Mark Gordon.

Artis puts his final signature on the game with a slam dunk; referee John Vanak has a great view. April 4, 1975. Photo by Mark Gordon.

The ABA became the first league in professional basketball to record blocked shots on the stat sheet. Artis goes high and knocks Larry Kenon's shot out-of-bounds. #22 Wil Jones ducks as Artis falls toward him. #24 Ted McClain and #44 Dan Issel were going to try and get the rebound. #32 Dr. J watches, but there is nothing he can do. April 4, 1975. Photo by Mark Gordon.

#53 Artis Gilmore secures his favorite spot on the floor… right side of the basket, low post. #25 Tom Owens and #4 Chuck Williams of the Sounds don't want to let him turn into the lane for his left-handed hook shot. Kentucky wins 98-91, as Artis pours in 25 points and 20 rebounds. April 6, 1975. Photo by Mark Gordon.

The Memphis Sounds' Tom Owens and Chuck Williams try to force Artis into a turnover in the 1975 ABA playoffs. Kentucky wins Game 5 behind Gilmore's 31 points and 20 rebounds 111-99. The Colonels win the series and move on to the Eastern Division Semi-Finals. April 13, 1975. Photo by Mark Gordon.

There is one thing that is certain…this best-of-seven series will be played "above the rim". Artis blocks #20 Maurice Lucas' shot. Also pictured #10 Louie Dampier, #24 Ted McClain, #44 Dan Issel, and referee Jack Madden. April 21, 1975. Photo by Mark Gordon.

Artis opens another bottle to share with Ron Thomas, celebrating their playoff victory over St. Louis in the playoffs. Artis had 29 points, 20 rebounds, and 7 blocked shots. April 28, 1975. Photo by Mark Gordon.

Press, radio, photographers, and sports writers swarm the court to view the presentation of the championship trophy to the Colonels owner Ellie Brown. May 22, 1975. Photo by Mark Gordon.

Kentucky faces the Buffalo Braves at home. Artis scored 36 points in 36 minutes, 17 in the last quarter, and 10 in the final 2:48 to revive the Colonels in time to win the game 120-116. October 14, 1975. Photo by Mark Gordon.

The night was bittersweet. Dan Issel, now with the Denver Nuggets, has come home to face his former teammates for the first time since John Y. Brown traded him on September 19. The trade dissolved the championship team. November 2, 1975. Photo by Mark Gordon.

1975-76, standing, left to right: General Manager David Vance, Jimmie Backer, Jan van Breda Kolff, Maurice Lucas, Artis Gilmore, Jim McDaniels, Wilbert Jones, Ron Thomas, trainer Lloyd Gardner, and Vice President of Operations Gene Rhodes. Seated: Johnny Neumann, Jimmy Dan Conner, Bird Averitt, assistant coach Stan Albeck, Ellie Brown, head coach Hubie Brown, Louie Dampier, Kevin Joyce, and Allen Murphy.

Kentucky Colonels Trophy and Championship Medallion, 1975. Courtesy of Kyle D. Eberle.

FINAL PLAYOFF SERIES, 1975

Championship Game No. 3

May 17, at Market Square, Indianapolis

KENTUCKY (109)

PLAYER	Pos.	Min.	2-Pt. FG-FGA	3-Pt. FG-FGA	FT-FTA	Rebounds O-D—T	A	E	PF	TP
Jones, Wilbert	F	17	0-2	0-0	0-0	1- 1— 2	3	2	4	0
Issel, Dan	F	43	9-18	0-0	8-10	7- 5—12	4	0	5	26
Gilmore, Artis	C	47	17-28	0-0	7-8	11-17—28	1	6	4	41
Dampier, Louie	G	41	6-10	0-3	1-1	0- 1— 1	3	2	1	13
McClain, Ted	G	37	3-10	0-0	4-4	0- 4— 4	7	4	2	10
Averitt. Bird	G	18	3-11	0-1	0-0	0- 0— 0	4	2	1	6
Roberts, Marv	F	31	6-14	0-0	1-1	4- 2— 6	5	0	4	13
Thomas, Ron	C-F	6	0-0	0-0	0-0	0- 1— 1	0	1	1	0
TOTALS		240	44-93	0-4	21-24	23-31—54	27	17	22	109

INDIANA (101)

PLAYER	Pos.	Min.	2-Pt. FG-FGA	3-Pt. FG-FGA	FT-FTA	Rebounds O-D—T	A	E	PF	TP
Knight, Billy	F	44	13-15	0-0	2-3	3- 9—12	5	3	2	28
McGinnis, George	F	26	7-11	0-5	5-7	4- 6—10	3	6	6	19
Hillman, Darnell	C	34	7-12	0-0	4-6	4- 4— 8	2	2	5	18
Buse, Don	G	37	3-10	1-1	0-0	2- 0— 2	5	1	1	9
Joyce, Kevin	G	35	5-9	0-0	2-2	0- 2— 2	2	2	4	12
Brown, Roger	F	9	0-2	0-0	2-2	1- 0— 1	2	1	3	2
Keller, Bill	G	24	2-6	0-5	0-0	0- 0— 0	3	1	0	4
Elmore, Len	G	31	4-9	0-0	1-1	1- 7— 8	4	2	4	9
TOTALS		240	41-71	1-11	16-21	15-28—43	26	18	25	101

Blocked shots—Gilmore, McGinnis, Hillman, Elmore, Joyce.

Steals—Jones, McClain 4, Issel, Dampier, Joyce, Hillman, Buse 2, Brown.

Kentucky	31	25	17	36 —109
Indiana	30	21	30	20 —101

Referees—John Vanak and Ed Middleton.

Technical foul—Kentucky, bench.

Attendance—17,388.

Box scores

#53 Artis Gilmore and Indiana Pacers #30 George McGinnis, #20 Darnell Hillman, and Kevin Joyce, and referee John Vanak.

Artis Gilmore and Pacers #30 George McGinnis.

Left to right: Wilt "The Stilt" Chamberlain, Artis Gilmore, All-Star MVP, Ray Scott, and East Team Coach Babe McCarthy.

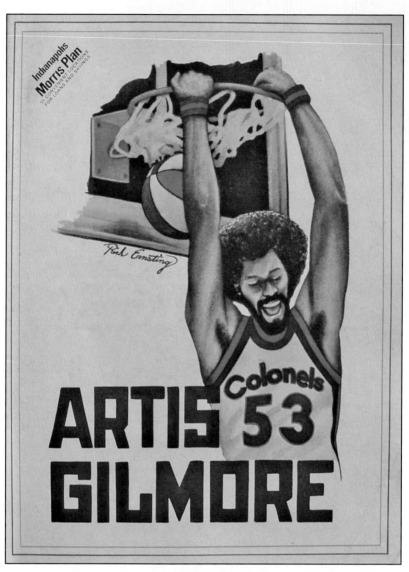

1975-76 Pacers Program

1976 **CHICAGO BULLS** 1977

Seated (L-R) John Mengelt, Wilbur Holland, Gene Tormohlen., Asst. Coach, Jon Kovler., Mng. Partner, Arthur Wirtz., Chmn. of Executive Committee, Coach Ed Badger, Trainer Doug Atkinson, Tom Kropp. Standing (L-R) John Laskowski, Scott May, Phil Hicks, Mickey Johnson, Artis Gilmore, Tom Boerwinkle, Cliff Pondexter, Jack Marin, Keith Starr. *Insert* Capt. Norm Van Lier

Chicago Bulls team photo, 1976-77 NBA season

Artis Gilmore in his first year with the Chicago Bulls, 1976-77.

Artis Gilmore playing for the Chicago Bulls.

Artis Gilmore during his first year with the Chicago Bulls, 1976-77.

WINNING

Winning requires no description. Although I eventually tasted and savored the American Basketball Association championship with the Kentucky Colonels in 1975, no ballplayer forgets his or her first true rush of victory. For me, this came in 1969-70, during my first year with the Dolphins of Jacksonville University.

After my second year at Gardner-Webb, I fortunately received interest from many schools. I visited Iowa, which was pretty good at the time, and I got to spend some time out there. But as I noted earlier, JU became my choice because it was closer to home. My parents were aging, so it gave me an opportunity to be near them, as well as my younger brothers and sisters.

Just by circumstance, my good friend and Gardner-Webb teammate Ernie Fleming also received a scholarship offer from JU. Gardner-Webb was in the process of converting to a four-year school and really wanted Ernie and me to stay. Ernie, however, had remembered how nice the JU coaches had been while recruiting him during high school. He wrote a three-page letter to JU coach Joe Williams and assistant coach (later head coach) Tom Wasdin, saying that he was interested in transferring. At the bottom it said: "P.S. I'd like to bring my roommate."

That was me.

Interestingly, although that got their attention, Coach Williams was reluctant to make the trip to Gardner-Webb to scout me. He basically told Coach Wasdin that he was exhausted from the process of looking at prospective new players and really didn't want to travel to North Carolina just to discover another slow guy who couldn't play.

Coach Wasdin kept after him, though, and the two attended a game in which I blocked shots left and right. Coach Williams said that within four minutes he was on his feet cheering. In short: the coaches liked me, I liked them, and it became a done deal. Over the years since then, Coach Wasdin has repeatedly paid me the compliment of replying to the question "To what do you contribute your success as a coach?" by saying: "Good luck, hard work, and Artis Gilmore."

At JU, we sensed our quality early in the year. The team had actually shown real promise the season before, beating top-ranked teams such as Georgia Tech and Florida State. We scrimmaged against Duke a few times. It was only practice, but we squashed them. A tiny school like ours running mighty Duke off the court was no small feat. We played a preseason game against Davidson, the No. 4 team in the country then, and took them apart. They had a great player named Mike Maloy, but we still smacked them by about 30 points. Around this time, Gene Pullen, a sports writer at the Jacksonville Journal, started predicting that JU had a real chance at winning the national title. Everyone else laughed. We believed it.

We also realized early on that the individuals on our team had a great relationship with each other. As any sports fan knows, it's not necessary for players to hang out off the court — or even like each other personally — in order to win championships. It is, of course, a lot more fun when you truly like each other, and we did. We all lived in the same dorm on the same floor. We would go to different events together. Our fraternities were very close. We played football together. It all had a "home away from home" feel. We had goofy nicknames for ourselves like the "Mod Squad" and were having the time of our lives.

The roster that year was:

Rusty Baldwin	Sophomore: 5' 10" Guard
Mike Blevins	Junior: 6' 5" Guard
Pembrook Burrows	Junior: 7' 0" Forward
Chip Dublin	Junior: 6' 0" Guard
Artis Gilmore	Junior: 7' 2" Center
Dan Hawkins	Senior: 6' 5" Guard
Curtis Kruer	Sophomore: 6' 5" Guard
Rod McIntyre	Senior: 6' 10" Forward/Center
Rex Morgan	Senior: 6' 5" Guard
Greg Nelson	Junior: 6' 6" Forward
Ken Selke	Senior: 6' 7" Forward
Vaughn Wedeking	Junior: 5' 10" Guard

You'll notice that we had a bit of size; both Pembrook Burrows and I measured 7 feet or taller. Rod McIntyre stood just shy of that mark. That was the tallest college team in the country and taller than most NBA teams at the time.

Rod was an excellent example of why we were such a close-knit team. Until my arrival, Rod started at center for JU for three years. Many guys would have jumped ship for another school or pouted about being relegated to the bench. Not Rod.

Although he didn't start playing basketball until ninth grade, he was an all-around great athlete. We had different skillsets that added different things to our team, and that made us all better. He handled the ball exceptionally well for a big guy, which gave us additional options for moving up and down the court, especially when other teams were pressing us. Rod realized that, at that point in my career, I was a low-post player, a rebounder, and a shot blocker. I was capable of putting up points, but he was quicker and could play a variety of positions.

That's exactly what happened. Rod played the high post, the 2-guard, and either forward position. He was always my friend and that reflected in the way he complemented my strengths and limitations on the court. Together, we destroyed our opposition!

In much the same way, Pembrook Burrows, our other 7-footer, felt no threat from me. He came over to the Dolphins that same summer from Brevard Community College and took the coach's word that, despite my arrival, he would see big playing time. Pembrook could be a bit of a character. At that time, there was a song called "The Rooster," which was part of some TV show. One day, after Coach Williams had been running us for quite a while, Pembrook got bored and started singing "The Rooster." It caught on and for a long time, whenever we felt like it, we'd all start singing "The Rooster." Of course, as time went on, the lyrics changed to ridiculous things like:

> *"Jacksonville had a rooster, and he sat on the fence. He crowed for the Dolphins, and he had good sense."*

Other lyrics probably should never be repeated. Eventually we used "The Rooster" as part of pregame warm-ups. It got just plain crazy with all sorts of "hidy hidy ho" stuff, but it got us all charged up and ready to play.

Greg Nelson came off the bench for Pembrook, and they were so good as a tandem we treated them like a single player. In fact, we referred to them as Pembrook Nelson. Between the two of them, we knew we could count on 20 points per game. Their respective averages were almost identical with Pembrook at 10.8 per game and Greg at 10.6. It has been proven time and time again that winning teams are made possible when everyone knows his role. That's what happened at JU, and that's why we were winners.

Vaughn Wedeking, for example, was the ideal point guard for us. One of only two guys shorter than six feet, he knew how to distribute the rock. He understood how others played their game and directed the action by maximizing what each of us did well individually. He was also willing and able to take the open shot when he got it.

On the defensive side of the floor we had Mike Blevins. Again: a winning team needs specialists, and Mike was ours. He almost always took the assignment of guarding the hottest offensive player on the opposing team. Every one of us had complete confidence that Mike, like a bulldog sinking his teeth in a victim's ankle, would not back off his enemy until the job was done.

To add a bit of streetball spice to life at JU, we had Chip Dublin. Chip came from New York City and brought with him the more freewheeling, cocky style of big city buckets. Yet Chip was anything but arrogant. In fact, he had an immediate smile and a warm, engaging way about him that made everyone feel happy to be in his presence. Coach Williams said he and Chip once gave a presentation at a downtown civic club where no black person had ever set foot. Chip, who indeed was black, felt comfortable even in that environment and made friends wherever he went.

Rex Morgan and I came to be known as Batman and Robin, I suppose because we were a bit of a dynamic duo. I averaged 26.5 points per game, and Rex put up an average of 18.2. I'm not sure that puts us in comic book superhero status, but it was good enough for plenty of wins. I remember promotional posters from that year showing Rex and me wearing colorful capes. I'm kind of glad that the imagery didn't follow into my professional years. At that time I was not yet known as "The A-Train" but as "The Big A" — a well-intentioned but questionable nickname that also, fortunately, didn't live beyond my time at JU.

To round us off, we had Joe Williams at the helm. Coach was not your typical old-school type guy. In fact, he was the perfect personality to lead a team of young men who knew they were good but wanted to stretch their abilities to see what else they could accomplish. He ran us through our drills, but he also allowed us to find our own levels, combinations, and styles. Even our pregame warm-ups, filled with "Sweet Georgia Brown" music and dunks (remember, you couldn't dunk during games then), were a stark contrast to the structured drills most teams would run. We wore mutton chop sideburns, beards, and fashionable blazers. Coach himself set an interesting fashion tone with his lucky jacket — a vanilla-looking outfit more befitting on top an ice cream cone. He claimed he wore it because I said I liked it. I'm not sure I ever said such a thing, but there's no doubt that Joe Williams' magic jacket contributed to our success.

Yet another key example of why we were winners had to do with the matter of race. Remember that this was 1969 and 1970, and lip service was given to integrating college sports, but many programs still were racially restrictive. I played on and against my first integrated teams only two years prior. At JU, we played large school teams that had not yet integrated or had made only obvious token efforts to appear as if they had done so. This was an unsettled time in our country's history, and civil rights were a focus of much debate and frequent violence.

Although this is a generalization, it seems as if the problem of race in sports doesn't involve the players as much as it does fans and the structure surrounding teams, such as ownership, management, and coaching staffs. The game itself, because of the physical and mental closeness it creates between players, often erases or at least dilutes racial attitudes and misconceptions. I know that is not always the case, but it certainly was with the 1969-70 Dolphins. We were proud to say that we were a team that "didn't see color."

Rod McIntyre remembers the story about one of the first times we ate together in a public cafe. Bear in mind that just a few years before, there would have been many restaurants that would not have allowed us to all sit down together, let alone eat with each other. Chip Dublin and one of the white guys mixed their drinks up. Both began drinking from the other's cup before they realized the mistake and then switched back. Although no one said anything, we all wondered the same thing: "Is this guy going to drink from that cup after a black guy had it and vice versa?" With us, the answer was: "Of course." That helped set the tone of unity for our team.

It may be difficult for some people today to understand how and why this small incident could be so important, but often it's the small things that point to larger realities. With that team, we also felt that our harmony as a group of athletes extended out into the campus, community, and beyond. We were a small team of white guys, black guys, tall guys, short guys, serious guys, and goofy guys, all who came together to drive a small school into the national spotlight. That energized Jacksonville and shed important light on what true brotherhood can accomplish.

Our winning season began with a bang on December 1, 1969. I poured in 35 points in an easy win over East Tennessee State. The next game, a lopsided 117-63 victory over Morehead State, went about the same.

Then, on December 18 against Georgetown, something unusual occurred. Arthur White, the Hoyas' leading scorer, punched Mike Blevins just before half time — probably because Mike got under his skin with great defense. Other guys started throwing punches, and Rex Morgan got nailed, as well. Fans began jumping into the action, and it escalated into a real riot for a while. After the break, Georgetown refused to take the court, so we won the game by forfeit. We always felt that, even though this was early in the year, our season began to turn at that very moment. Our tiny school had become a giant slayer. That was also the last game we could play on our original home court at Swisher Gym because our fans had outgrown the capacity. From then on, we played at the much larger Jacksonville Coliseum.

At the close of the calendar year, we won the Evansville Invitational, and I was fortunate enough to receive MVP recognition after scoring 32 against Arizona and 37 against Evansville. By early January, we had won our seventh game of the season while scoring 100 points, and the Associated Press moved us to No. 7 in the nation. Our tiny school was in the top 10 in the entire country! That resulted in the Coliseum being sold out for the first time in history, a fact that Rex Morgan personally celebrated by scoring 29 points in a 121-87 blowout of Miami. Six days later, Rex dropped 32 more in a 114-66 drubbing of the Virgin Islands.

On January 27, the other shoe dropped, and we suffered our only regular season loss at the hands of Florida State. Ironically, Hugh Durham, who later became one of the most successful coaches in Jacksonville University history, coached the Seminoles at this time. As I mentioned before, this was the only college game my mother could attend, and she blamed herself for the loss. I couldn't convince her that Florida State's great Dave Cowens might have had something to do with it rather than any jinx.

After six more Dolphins victories, we met Florida State again and returned the favor, beating them 85-81 on our home court. Coach Williams started Pembrook Burrows and me as the "twin towers" to out-muscle Dave Cowens. However, Chip Dublin was the real hero, scoring 14 points (nearly twice his per-game average) as one of five players in double figures.

I would like to publicly thank Coach Durham, who I first met during the contests against Florida State, for his many years of kind words and support of my career. Coach Durham has called me the most dominant college player in the country during my time at JU and even called me a "good guy" on top of it all. I appreciate his generosity about my abilities but am even more grateful that I have earned his respect as a person.

After three more victories, we were poised to join March Madness and vie for the national championship. Coach Williams had been waiting nervously by the phone for the call from the NCAA. Some folks believed that despite our record, we would not receive an invitation because we were a small, relatively unknown independent school. But in the end, our achievements trumped the name. The

1969-70 Dolphins became the first team in the nation to average more than 100 points per game, which led to a great scoring margin of 21.9. I led the nation in rebounding with 22.2 rebounds per game and also chipped in 26.5 points per game.

By this time, the entire city of Jacksonville had risen behind us, and the excitement was, to use a cliché, almost thick enough to taste. Our first national exposure came on March 7 in Dayton, Ohio, as we beat Western Kentucky 109-96 in our first-ever nationally televised appearance. I had a 30-point, 19-rebound game, and Rex added 24 points. This was also the beginning of the public association of my name, Artis Gilmore, with the hairstyle popularly known as the Afro. It's been said, probably truthfully, that I was 7' 2" naturally, but 7' 6" with my full Afro.

Jim McDaniels, an All-American who led the Western Kentucky Hilltoppers, paid me a very kind compliment, saying:

> *I don't think we really were aware we were running into a buzz saw. The game starts and Artis Gilmore came out with that big Afro, and it scared you to death because he was just such a big guy. After looking at Artis Gilmore, I just seriously went into prayer. Once we started playing, they really could play. We really didn't realize how good they were, but it really didn't take very long to find out. Against Artis Gilmore, you just couldn't get a lay up. Without a doubt he is just a tremendous athlete, physically, and all the way around. He is one of the strongest athletes I'd ever played against.*

Five days later, we went up against Iowa in Columbus, Ohio, and our ride almost ended right then and there. First, Vaughn Wedeking was sick as a dog with the flu. Second, Rex Morgan had an ear infection. And, third, I got a bit too aggressive on defense and fouled out with eight minutes left in the game. A last-second tip-in by Pembrook Burrows off a missed shot by Vaughn gave us a 104-103 squeaker over the Hawkeyes. Rex Morgan takes every opportunity, even now, to remind me that I almost cost the team the game by fouling out at a crucial moment. He's fond of recalling how I sat on the bench trying to coach Pembrook. According to Rex, I said, "Pembrook, listen, man, you really have to make this thing happen," to which Pembrook replied, "I guess so, man, you're sitting on the bench!"

Two days later, we faced Kentucky in what is one of the single most memorable wins of my career. Kentucky: No. 1 in the nation. Kentucky: a legendary basketball powerhouse. Kentucky: coached by Adolph Rupp. Rupp is one of the winningest coaches in college basketball history but was also a man of highly question-able racial tolerance. In 1966, after his Wildcats became the first all-white college team to be defeated by an all-black starting five (Texas Western), Rupp supposedly and begrudgingly referred to black athletes and said, "I guess I got to get me some of them." Whether or not that was actually verbatim, Rupp had come to symbol-ize racial attitudes of a certain type of coach. Even among more "tolerant" bench managers of that time, the not-so-funny joke about when to use black players went "Two blacks at home. Three on the road. Four when behind in the game." The long and short of it was whether it was a black JU Dolphin player or a white one, we really wanted to put the hurt on Kentucky. Really and truly.

For that game, Kentucky was still fielding an all-white team, but I point that out only as a matter of historical interest. I absolutely do not intend to take anything away from the quality of their team led by Hall-of-Famer Dan Issel, a phenomenal player who would eventually become my teammate with the Ken-tucky Colonels. Five years later, Dan and I would win an ABA championship together, but on March 14, 1970, we were enemies.

Kentucky felt as strongly about us as we did about them. Coach Rupp didn't like our long hair or swagger. Who were we, a small school with no basketball pedigree, to think we could stand up to the mighty and talented Kentucky? To give you an idea of how personal this game became, there was a moment late in the game when one of the Kentucky players pulled a trick on me by running across my path, then stopping dead in his tracks, so I would crash into him. That's exactly what happened, and I picked up a dangerous third foul. Most of the fans there were from Kentucky, and they went wild with cheering. On the very next play on the other side of the court, Vaughn Wedeking did the very same thing to Dan Issel, putting a foul on him. Vaughn normally showed little facial emotion on the court and said nearly nothing, but as he ran by the Kentucky bench, he yelled at Adolph Rupp: "That was for you, old man!" Not very respectful, I guess, but we were not out there to respect Kentucky or its coach. We won the game 106-100. I had 24 points, and Rex Morgan had 28. We were met by tens of thousands of fans lining the streets when we returned to Jacksonville.

We were now in the famous NCAA Final Four in College Park, Maryland. We were only one win away from the NCAA championship game but needed to get by St. Bonaventure. We did so by a score of 91-83. In this game, we caught a break because St. Bonaventure's great Bob Lanier could not play due to an injured knee. Rex Morgan claims to this day that it wouldn't have mattered any-way, but that's Rex being Rex. Bob was an amazing talent, and with him playing, the game would have been tough. Bob and I have become good friends over the years, but I still feel it necessary to take Rex's side of the argument and needle Bob every chance about how no one even missed him!

On March 21, 1970, Jacksonville University met the UCLA Bruins, who had won three consecutive national championships, in the NCAA finals. That, however, is a story I will save for the next chapter.

As an individual player, my time at Jacksonville University is a time remembered for how wonderful it felt to grow almost daily in terms of skill levels.

- All-time NCAA Division I career rebounding average leader (22.7 rebounds per game)
- One of only eight players in college history to average 20 points and 20 rebounds per game over a career.
- Elected to the NCAA All-Tournament Team (1970) and the National Association of Basketball Coaches All-American Team (1970-71).
- NCAA rebounding champion in 1970 and 1971.
- Jacksonville University retired my jersey, No. 53, in 1992.

And yet, it is the overall accomplishment of our team, the 1969-70 Jacksonville University Dolphins, that gives me the most pride. For the first time in my life, I truly learned what it felt like to be a winner. We finished our season with a 27-2 record and a perfect home record of 13-0. Yes, we finished as NCAA runner-ups. And, yes, it is often said that no one remembers who finished second. I'm here to tell you, however, that many people remember the winners who were the 1969-70 Dolphins. We rose from nowhere to beat and compete against the legends of college basketball. We galvanized a university, a city, and a whole lot of basketball fans who were pulling for the underdog. At times, there was so much excitement in Jacksonville that we had to travel with a police escort to get through the crowds. It was an extraordinary time.

Sports are obviously about winning. Winning often translates into money, power, fame, and glory. An athlete's first big experience with winning is considerably simpler. Maybe it can be compared to a first love. In that sense, winning is pure. It's that peculiar warmth and calmness even when surrounded by wild excitement.

That first time came at Jacksonville University and left me understanding that winning need not — maybe cannot — be completely described. Nor does it need to be described to be completely understood.

LOSING

There's no need to be philosophical about winning. An athlete lives to win. There's nothing better. End of story.

Losing?

Well, losing is the stuff of long, late night deep-thinking conversations. Losses live in the world of unanswerable questions, unprovable guesses, and endless regrets based on the 20/20 vision of hindsight.

I've had my shares of losses.

You can learn from losses; in fact, some losses are tremendous learning lessons and highly motivating. But some losses are just irritating!

When I was playing, I had the reputation of being the strongest player in professional basketball, except for Wilt Chamberlain. Phil Jackson — the world-class coach, former New York Knicks enforcer, and now president of the Knicks — has been quoted as saying, "Artis was probably the strongest person who has ever played the game." I appreciate the compliment, but I'll gladly admit that Chamberlain was stronger. I had the privilege of playing against him only once, in an ABA/NBA All-Star Game in 1972. I was closer to the beginning of my career; Chamberlain at the end of his. Especially in the first half, I did pretty well against the old lion, but believe me when I say that you could feel his power even when he didn't touch you. He was fond of putting a young guy's butt down hard on the floor early in the game just to set the tone and remind everyone who was the boss.

Chamberlain, however, was not a mean-spirited man, and despite his great strength, he was in very few fights over his many years on the court. I was the same way. I felt no need to prove myself with my fists. I was a basketball player, not a boxer, and although I enjoyed the physical contact of the low post game, which could become very brutal and bruising, I saw no reason to throw punches at the first opportunity.

That fact haunted me in one instance. During a game against the St. Louis Spirits, tempers did flare up. The result was that Maurice Lucas, who was then a rookie, punched me right in the jaw. Maurice was a strong man who, unlike me, enjoyed a good brawl and landed a solid shot. Believe me, I felt it from my head to the end of my sneakers. I think my knees may have gone in a few different directions. Over the years this story has grown, and I had supposedly chased Maurice around the arena until, when cornered, he put my lights out with one swift jab. Well, that's a fair amount more dramatic and fantastical than what really happened. However, it does highlight one of the realities of living life at 7' 2" and (at that time) 240 pounds. Had I clobbered Maurice, it would have either been a non-news story, or I would have been cast in the role of the big bully picking on a smaller man.

Being as large as I was definitely gave me an advantage on the basketball court, but I do sympathize with other big centers, like Shaquille O'Neal, who didn't get the same calls a guard would get. I know how Shaq feels — we definitely took our share of punishment in the paint and just had to deal with it.

As it was, some accounts claim that the incident made Maurice so confident that it contributed to his career-long success as a player. If my chin gave an assist to Maurice, I'm happy. He was a great guy. I doubt, though, that this had much to do with his many great years as a player. Maurice was pretty damn good to start with.

Not being the heavyweight champion of the world is a loss that I can easily live with. Others are tougher to take.

Two of the best years of my life were 1969 and 1970 when, as part of the Jacksonville University basketball team, I enjoyed a hugely successful season filled with winning. The Dolphins won all but one game during the regular season. As I detailed in the previous chapter, I was then fortunate enough to play in the NCAA tournament final. But … we lost.

Life presents interesting contrasts, doesn't it? A team wins everything — except the last game. Does that make it a winning season — or a lost tournament — or can the two exist independently of each other?

In the final chapter of this book, I talk about why the 1969-70 season remains a huge win in my mind despite the final game's loss. Now, however, I want to talk about the importance of that one game, that one loss.

The date was March 21, 1970. The place was College Park, Maryland. Our opponents: UCLA under the tutelage of the legendary John Wooden. UCLA had won three straight NCAA titles and would go on to win three more after this season. This was smack dab in the middle of the Bruins dynasty in which UCLA won the title 10 out of 12 years.

Were we intimidated? Not in the least. *Sports Illustrated* reported that I was so relaxed that I fell asleep in a hotel lobby chair before our first practice. That was true. But that was not a sign that we took the game lightly. UCLA was synonymous with powerhouse basketball, and even though the phenomenal Kareem Abdul-Jabbar had graduated the year before, Coach Wooden retained a starting five that each averaged double-digit scoring: Sidney Wicks at 18.6, John Vallely 16.3, Henry Bibby 15.6, Curtis Rowe 15.3, and Steve Patterson 12.5. They averaged 92 points a game for the season and scored 133 points against an LSU team led by "Pistol" Pete Maravich.

We got off to a great start in the game, quickly jumping out to a 14-6 lead. I was guarded by Wicks, who later went on to a very successful 10-year NBA career, averaging 16.8 points and nearly nine rebounds per game. Wicks began by guarding me from the side, but at 6' 8" he was physically unable to contain me, and I scored three quick, easy baskets on the inside.

You may recall the phrase I used in the opening chapter of this book: ***The great ones create.*** It was at this point in the game the creative greatness of John Wooden demonstrated itself. Coach Wooden called a timeout and redesigned the UCLA defense. Instead of positioning Wicks to my side, Coach Wooden moved him directly behind me. Steve Patterson and others then began to slack off their own men to guard me on either side.

Coach Wooden later explained that his tactic was to make sure that if and when I got inside and down low close to the basket, there would be a maximum number of hands and arms in my way, making it crowded and difficult for me to move properly. He was correct.

With this new defensive plan in place, Wicks was freer to focus on obstructing my actual shots and blocked five shots during the game. These blocks have always been a bit of a sore spot with Jacksonville supporters, who believe that most of them were actually goaltending and should have counted as points made. At a dinner many years later that I attended with fellow Dolphins, members of the UCLA squad, and Coach Wooden, John Vallely kicked off the evening by saying: "Let's get this out of the way, Sidney goaltended Artis."

Andy Hill, John's UCLA teammate, added: "At least four times."

Maybe they said it because they believed it. Maybe they're nice guys and wanted me to feel better. As for me, I really don't look back and judge the game by what it may have been. Wicks played an excellent game, and he played aggressively. In basketball, calls tend to go in favor of the team that is the most aggressive. That's always the way it's been.

The lesson of this loss wasn't immediately clear. Like any young man, I was not happy with the loss. I shot only 9-for-29, scoring 19 points and grabbing

16 rebounds. That was well below my season average of 26.5 points and 22.2 rebounds. I fouled out with 1:50 left on the clock, and we fell by a final score of 80-69. I had the added displeasure of seeing Sidney and myself on the cover of the next *Sports Illustrated* with the headline: **"Wicks Outrebounds Gilmore."**

Was my pride hurt? Of course. But eventually the lesson began to sink in: Adaptability is a key to winning, but it is also a key to turning a loss into a personal strength. Coach Wooden, because he was a truly great coach, "created" a victory by being adaptable. He changed the UCLA defense when it wasn't working. Some coaches panic during the big moments because they refuse to deviate from their core beliefs and game plan. Coach Wooden got even better precisely because he had an open mind and adapted his original strategy.

Everything in life is a series of minor and not-so-minor adjustments to the constant changes around us. I was able to adapt my mind to this loss and to other losses in my life because I now realize that careers and lives are not defined by a single game. Seen through the light of the years, my pride in our triumphs of 1969-70 truly and substantially outweighs the disappointment of one night in March. We were a team from a school with an enrollment of only a few thousand, and we went to the very final minutes against institutions with legendary histories in basketball and tens of thousands of students from which to build winning basketball teams.

Nothing in my life has lessened my competitive spirit to win. I get steamed during pickup games when my team loses. Yet, lessons gained from brutal, hard-to-swallow losses have, I believe, given me an added perspective. It concerns me when I hear about coaches and parents mentally — and sometimes physically — abusing young athletes because of a real or imagined contribution to a losing effort.

Here's the reality of sports, and, for that matter, of life: Everyone loses. Everyone loses games. Everyone loses friends. Everyone loses loved ones. No one has to accept loss easily. No one should stop trying to win. But everyone needs to learn from the hidden benefits that can come from not winning. How this happens is very individualized. I can't tell you how to do it for yourself except to say that being realistic about the roles that winning and losing play in one's ability to be happy is the first step to achieving that happiness.

Let me share one more loss with you. I've been able to live with this one without much problem. During my days with the Kentucky Colonels in the ABA, I had the pleasure of meeting many celebrities. One whose original home was in Louisville, Kentucky, was a gentleman by the name of Muhammad Ali.

Ali was not a man who lost easily. Early in his remarkable career, he said, "I'm gonna have to be killed before I lose, and I ain't gonna die easy." Muhammad

Ali was a fan of the Kentucky Colonels and took in a number of games when we played at home. One evening at halftime, while a television crew interviewed me, "The Champ" poked his head into the shot and challenged me to a fight.

Some of you may recall a similar exchange between Ali and Wilt Chamberlain. The difference was that Ali and Chamberlain just posed with their fists extended at each other until the cameras stopped clicking. With me, he began to pop me on the arm, goofing around, and talking nonstop. With each jab, though, the punches got harder and harder. I was trying to answer the reporter's questions while playing along with Muhammad Ali as he steadily set about to smack the hell out of me. He was the man famous for "floating like a butterfly, stinging like a bee," but that night I floated pretty quickly myself — to the safety of the Colonels' locker room.

My sore arm has long since healed, and I have no problem admitting that I lost to the Greatest Ever in our one-and-only courtside heavyweight fight. Moreover, I will always admire the way Muhammad Ali handled his own defeats when they eventually came. He summed up the reality of losing in a statement made after his second professional loss to Ken Norton. "I never thought of losing," he said, "but now that it's happened, the only thing is to do it right. That's my obligation to all the people who believe in me."

Ali passed away in 2016, and that was one of the biggest losses for the world. He changed the perception of athletes, particularly African-American athletes, in this country and led social change in an era that sorely needed it.

RULES

This chapter is for basketball players and for those who actually have learned their left from right feet. Until you truly know the fundamentals of the game, you better live by the rules of the game. If you don't, at best you'll be lucky to look only a bit foolish. At worst, you'll look like a clown who simply can't win. Only when you know the game will the rules become a true friend to you. Then you'll know how to bend them and get away with it. Sometimes.

The "Golden Rule," someone once said, really means "those with the gold make the rules." In basketball, as in society, it does sometimes seem like those with the most make the rules. Even powerful individual players are not above the rules made by those with the gold. Sure, superstars are allowed a little room within the rules. If Michael Jordan took an extra step or two, it could be overlooked because for most of the time he was flying rather than touching the ground. If Shaq puts down a shoulder and reduces his opponent to a flopping pile of hurt, an offensive foul may not be whistled. After all, "Might Makes Right" when playing in the low post. No rule enforcer would lean toward penalizing Shaq for not politely asking permission to rip the rim down!

From a historical perspective, it can be argued, rules are not as ironclad as they might seem or at least they are evolutionary. Don't forget: the original 13 rules of basketball as created by Dr. James Naismith in 1891 mainly apply to passing the ball and say absolutely nothing about dribbling. Although rules are intended to allow the game to grow to its greatest performance level, the rules themselves have occasionally been changed because some of history's greatest basketball players exceeded the limits of those rules. George Mikan, the NBA's first true big man and later commissioner of the ABA, would camp his 6' 10" body in the lane and was so dominant as a result that the paint area around the basket was widened and defensive goaltending was deemed illegal to give other players a chance.

When Wilt Chamberlain was in high school, he would "shoot" free throws by standing several feet behind the line, toss the ball in the air, run and jump toward the rim, and dunk it. Rule changes stopped this. As we all know, Chamberlain's ability to shoot a conventional free throw was not, to put it politely, a thing of beauty. The NCAA's so-called "Alcindor Rule" prohibited dunking for a number of years at the college level. People felt that players like Kareem Abdul-Jabbar, formerly Lew Alcindor, could dunk at will and would, therefore, be unstoppable.

Those are matters related to "official" rules. In basketball, there has always been a second set of rules — PLAYER RULES! Those might best be known from the highly publicized "Jordan Rules," a pre-planned but unofficial defensive strategy used by the Detroit Pistons against Michael Jordan in order to contain him. The *30 for 30* film about the Bad Boy Pistons describes these "rules" as a way to: "play him [Jordan] tough, to physically challenge him, and to vary its defenses so as to try to throw him off balance." Well, that's the delicate way to put it. A more accurate way would be to say "The 'Jordan Rules' were designed to beat the hell out of Michael Jordan." At first, the plan worked. We all know what happened later. M.J. ultimately played and won by his own rules.

One interesting fact about rules is that sometimes even the worst ones can have a silver lining. I just mentioned the "Alcindor Rule" against dunking. That rule affected me throughout my college career. As a result, players like myself who normally would have benefited from being able to dunk were forced to improve our other fundamentals, including inside footwork and, in my case, a soft left-handed hook. Kareem's beautiful skyhook resulted from this bad rule and his personal game — as well as the entire game of basketball — benefited greatly.

As I stated in the beginning of the chapter, a knowledgeable basketball player can make the rules a reliable friend. Again, I am talking only about basketball. I am not encouraging a life of crime in society, just hinting that ballplayers can have a little extra fun and further improve their game by recognizing that rules can bend without breaking.

I don't know how this applies to guards and forwards because I've never been a short guy and have never seen how the world looks from down there. From deep in the paint, though, I can tell you that many of the rules of basketball end at about the belly button. Refs are great about seeing what happens above the waist, but when the ball goes up toward the basket and all eyes follow it up, that's when big men start to have fun with the rules.

Hardly anyone, for example, ever sees how effective it is to wait until your opponent is about to jump for a rebound and then grab his wrist. His vertical leap just won't be the same. Nor will his attitude!

Very few people will ever notice when you grab your opponent quickly above the hip joint and give it a good hard squeeze. I guarantee that your opponent will notice, but by that time you've either thrown his game off balance mentally and physically or you've made your move around him.

And how about the old-school jersey pull? Very hard to detect, but if you are doing your job correctly, your opponent should leave the game defeated and in need of ironing a badly wrinkled jersey. I've even read where the true artists of rule bending will try to throw their opponent's game off by reaching down and plucking the hairs off the other guy's legs. For many reasons, I've never tried that one out!

Please realize that I'm being a little bit tongue-in-cheek about all of this. A little. Actually, one of the best compliments I ever received was from my old enemy but now longtime friend, Hall-of-Fame center Bill Walton. Bill said that while I might not have been the best player he ever played against (Kareem was), I gave him more trouble than anyone else. He then went on to say that I apparently had no understanding that things like double dribbles, three seconds in the lane, and offensive fouls were actually violations against the rules of basketball — and sometimes against the rules of human decency.

That makes me feel good. Obviously bending the rules against Walton worked at least a couple of times. In response to his accusation that I was unaware that rules actually exist, I say to him what I've always said while playing basketball against my oldest son, Otis James, a good-sized guy at 6' 10" and about 275 pounds. When he was younger, we would play one-on-one, and he would constantly complain that I stood in the lane, under the basket, for more than three seconds. "That's against the rules!" he'd gripe, to which I would always reply, and would still respond today: "When you're strong enough to move me out of the lane, then *you* can make the rules."

REBOUNDING

Rebounding is a part of basketball that, like many parts of life itself, is something a person either just gets or doesn't get. To win in basketball, you need to have possession of the ball. Plain and simple. Securing the ball via rebounding is one of the keys to success on the hardwood. For most big men, rebounding is the key to even getting on the court.

In life, each of us is constantly faced with the need to bounce back or rebound from any number of challenges. The same is true in hoops. I know that the symbolic comparison may seem overly simplistic, but I think there's more to it than may meet the eye.

In basketball, being a good rebounder does not depend on being the tallest player on the court. Height is certainly an advantage, but in numerous instances, a team's top rebounder is not the tallest. Dennis Rodman, who has frequently been cited as one of the game's best rebounding specialists, is perhaps the most obvious and profoundly successful example at 6' 7." Ben Wallace, 6' 9," is another good example of an undersized center with great rebounding skills who was used to beating out taller men. Of course, I can't forget Charles Barkley, the 6' 6" forward nicknamed "The Round Mound of Rebound," who averaged 11.7 boards per game. There is an old saying in our game: rebounding happens most of the time below the rim. This is true even at the professional level.

There are many reasons why a player becomes a good rebounder, some of which I'll discuss in a moment. Foremost among them is this cold hard fact: To be a good rebounder you have to *want* to be a good rebounder. That is, you have to constantly desire to secure the basketball.

This may not be as obvious to many as you may think. You might ask yourself: "Why would anyone *not* want to be a good rebounder?" The answer is that it requires a certain mindset and a definite commitment to certain irrefutable rules.

Rule One: Rebounding is a dirty job.

Some players are white-collar guys. That's neither good nor bad — it's just the way it is. Those players want to play their game from a safe distance, using their shooting skills, ball-handling abilities, and court vision for pinpoint passing and foot speed for finesse. I'm not just talking about guards. The rise of the "stretch 4" takes many big men away from the basket, and they simply do not have a taste for the art of rebounding, which, by its nature, means banging heads and butts with guys who are as large as trucks and as mean as pit bulls. It means abandoning all caution to go for the basketball, totally aware that at any given time a sharp elbow can find your temple, a forearm can crush your throat, your opponent can grab your wrist and pull you to the floor, or your shorts may be pulled halfway down your legs! Ballplayers who *want* to rebound love the sweat, the intense contact, and the unbeatable feeling of a working man's accomplishment of coming out of the jaws of death holding the ball. As a true competitor, I always want to win in everything I do, and each rebound I secured felt like a small victory.

Rule Two: To be a good rebounder, you must be aware of the game within the game.

This means that you must always follow the larger flow of action. What play is being run? What are the patterns? What is your responsibility? What are your teammates doing? Where will each of your teammates be? What is the guy you are guarding doing? What are the other opposing players up to? What are the second and third options? All those considerations are awareness of the game itself. None of those factors can be forgotten when a shot goes up, but a great rebounder must, as the ball is released, adjust to a game within the game — specifically, the rebounder must figure out how to get the ball off the boards without compromising other game-related priorities.

Most importantly, at this point in the process of rebounding, a good rebounder keeps his awareness of where the ball is at all times. If you watch 10 guys playing ball, you'll notice that when a shot is released, many players will turn toward the basket in an effort to get a rebound, but many do not follow the path of the ball itself. The result is that such players get rebounds only when they are lucky enough to be standing directly where the ball comes off the rim or backboard. A lot of players say they're interested in rebounding, but really they mean if the ball happens to be in their immediate rebound radius. A great rebounder calculates the flight of the ball and adjusts position accordingly. At this point, being tall — or being extremely strong — can certainly be a great advantage but only if that advantage is used. A small, weak man can hold back a huge, powerful man long enough to steal a rebound if he has the proper position.

I have heard people say that speed is essential to good rebounding, but I would argue that it's not speed but quickness in the ability to find the best possible position on the court. In turn, quickness is only as good as the awareness that tells a great rebounder, in a split second, that he should move this way or that way to optimize his chances of getting the ball.

Rule Three: Don't forget the laws of physics.

After all, a human player only has a finite amount of control over what happens in the effort to rebound. The behavior of the basketball itself influences almost everything else. For young players truly wanting to become reliable rebounders, let me underscore how important it is for you to study how other players, on your team and those against you, tend to shoot the ball.

For example, if a guy loves to shoot an angle shot, using the backboard to make off-the-glass buckets, you need to remember that when he misses, it is likely that the rebound will come off the opposite side in a corresponding angle. If another player shoots with a lot of arc, a missed shot will probably pop up high around the basket. Who shoots hard? Who shoots soft? The answers to those questions are clues as to where a good rebounder should begin the positioning process.

Also, knowing *when* someone is likely to shoot is equally important. We all know players who will shoot every time they get the ball. That may irritate other players, but a good rebounder will use that to his advantage. He will anticipate the probable shot and will get in position to clean up some easy garbage if the shot misses.

The underlying reality here is that it is not always possible to get the best position for a rebound. At those times, it is necessary to think about physics. Statistically, for example, a ball shot from the baseline, if it misses, is almost equally likely to bounce back toward the shooter or bounce straight away toward the opposite baseline side of the rim. Very infrequently will it ricochet out from the front of the rim. What is the message there? If you are on offense and your man has you blocked out on a baseline shot, don't try to fight what will probably be a losing battle for the position he already has. Move directly opposite him because there is a 50/50 chance that a missed baseline shot will come that direction. Angled shots, as I've mentioned, are statistically likely to rebound off the opposite side and in a similar angle pattern. The further out a straight-on ball is shot, the further out it is likely to carom off the rim. Of course, none of these likelihoods is a certainty, but understanding statistical probabilities gives the smart rebounder a real edge.

Although rebounding came easy to me, I always reminded myself to be alert for ways to improve. Beyond the obvious, rebounding was, to my way of thinking, not only a key element for victory but also something to concentrate on during shooting slumps and when other parts of the game just weren't going as well as I'd like. I'm pleased with the results:

- All-time NCAA Division I career rebounding average leader (22.7 rebounds per game)
- One of only eight players in college history to average 20 points and 20 rebounds per game over a career
- NCAA rebounding champion in 1970 and 1971
- Four-time ABA rebounding champion (1972-74, 1976)
- ABA regular-season single-game record of 40 rebounds versus New York: February 3, 1974
- Led Chicago Bulls in rebounding in three consecutive seasons and four overall (1976-78, 1981)
- Fifth-highest rebounder in pro basketball (ABA/NBA) history (16,330)
- Ranked in the top 10 in rebounding in 12-of-17 ABA/NBA seasons

This gets us back to my original effort to draw a parallel between rebounding the basketball and rebounding from low points in one's personal life. In each case it's a matter of trying, as much as possible, to ignore the distractions and to focus on what really matters. In the case of sports: your skills. In the case of life: the qualities that make you a good human being. That's how you get your head back in either game.

For me, that was the way to not only overcome big losses on the court but also to keep going night after night for 670 straight games, some of which were bruising, disheartening defeats.

It also helped me overcome a pretty grim childhood. As I've tried to make clear before, I'm no one special in terms of growing up poor, but the fact remains that a person can choose to feel sorry and stay underprivileged or a person can position for a rebound into a better life. Similarly, I have used that approach in successfully staying away from some of the problems that professional athletes fall prey to. I avoided drugs, even though they were readily available. The fact that controlled substances never were a part of who I am caused me some embarrassment in 2006 when I was cited for driving under the influence of alcohol after flipping my car. I was lucky to not have been killed and even luckier to not have injured anyone else, but I must admit that rebounding from that incident was as much of a challenge as anything I've faced on the basketball court. It was not reflective of who I am or what I stand for. In life, as in basketball, an isolated mistake can make a big difference in what happens next. That's a lesson that I hope to share with others as a way of helping them avoid similar risks.

A couple years earlier, in 2004, I had an even more personal need to rebound, and that was the death of my mother with whom I was very close. That was the single most profound sadness I have felt as a person. On a related note, perhaps the most profound sadness I felt as a professional athlete is that I wasn't inducted into the Basketball Hall of Fame until 2011, after my mother had passed, so she was not with me to share the achievement and joy. Yet this is the nature of both life and loss. And this is why I believe all of us are capable of being great rebounders — if we truly want to be and are willing to work hard at it.

To all who need to become better rebounders, on or off the court, I have this to say: Stay focused. Continue to work hard. Positive things will happen.

SWEATING THE SMALL STUFF

A few years ago, a book titled *Don't Sweat The Small Stuff ... and It's All Small Stuff* by Richard Carslson became very popular. I suppose that not sweating the small things is good advice for most people for most occasions, but success in professional sports is surely an exception to the rule.

The 1974-75 ABA season was one of the most successful times in my career. In 1975, the Kentucky Colonels won it all. In doing so, we not only sweated the small stuff, but we sweated ... and sweated ... and sweated. The reason can be explained in three words: Hubert Jude Brown.

Hubie Brown, who was just 41 years old at the time, had been hired away from the Milwaukee Bucks, where he was an assistant coach. Hubie believed in the old saying, "The devil is in the details." To him, small stuff mattered because small stuff tends to add up. He is absolutely correct.

Think of how many times a game is decided by "little" things. A guy is a little more tired than the man he is guarding. A player loses his concentration just a little bit and misses a box out. A free throw is missed or made because the shooter spent a little less or a little more time practicing earlier that week.

Earlier in the book, I told the story of my Jacksonville University team's NCAA championship game against UCLA when Coach John Wooden made a small change. He moved Sidney Wicks from his defensive stance in front of me to directly behind me, enabling two other UCLA players to complete a triple team box against me. This was a "small stuff" decision but one that had huge results during the course of the game.

Hubie Brown understood that, in basketball, you *must* sweat the small stuff if you expect to win. Especially for a head coach, it was his job to get in the weeds in preparation to make sure everything from the pre-game routine to the defensive rotations was just right. Every so often someone comes into your life and changes it. Coach Brown changed my entire mental approach to the game.

First of all, Hubie eats, drinks, and breathes basketball. It's his life and his passion. I think that's important in recognizing that the small stuff *is* important. If you are not passionate about something, you simply see no reason to look below the surface. Hubie not only looked beneath the surface, but he also dug like an archaeologist. He was a very detail-oriented coach, and as a result, when we competed against other teams, he had statistics and reports about many of the things that were successful against those particular squads. In a sense, he was ahead of his time by having such detailed scouting reports. If you think I'm exaggerating about that last comment, bear in mind that a few years earlier the coaching staff of the Cleveland Cavaliers had admitted to making expansion draft choices based on statistics on the back of basketball trading cards.

When I first joined the Colonels, we had great talent but couldn't quite get over the hump to win the championship. What Hubie taught me is that a team can have all the talent in the world, but if it doesn't execute, it can't win. Executing plays all boils down to mastering the small stuff, especially under pressure.

Some people can't understand why coaches — Bobby Knight is a great example — will yell at a player for being out of position by a few inches. The reason why is that those few inches can not only impact the success or failure of how that individual player competes against the other individual guarding or attacking him, but it can also greatly impact the flow of *all* other players around him.

Until Coach Brown came along, my primary offensive position on the floor was in the low post on the right box. Almost immediately, Hubie said I was too mobile to stay rooted in the same place that I had played throughout high school, college, and the pros. He had me move low, high, and even out into the wing area. It was sort of a precursor to all the floor stretching that's so in vogue now. I want to point out that, while many pundits today lament the extinction of the true big man, there have been mobile, jump-shooting bigs for decades. Willis Reed, Dave Cowens, Elvin Hayes, Rick Barry, Bob Lanier, even the great Bill Russell — they all had aspects to their games that weren't strictly back-to-the-basket.

At the time, moving around was new to me, but it opened my eyes to some great offensive opportunities. Additionally, it broadened my range in positioning for rebounds. In terms of the entire team, the fact that I was moving more meant that we benefited from extra patterns. If the play we ran was initially stopped, we would still have counters and other options to go to after that.

Coach Brown's attention to the small details all revolved around supporting two main theories about achieving basketball success. First: he believed that the best way to keep a player happy is to give him playing time. Makes sense, right? On many teams, however, only about eight guys typically see playing time. Hubie came in and began using a 10-man rotation. That's fairly common these days, but it was another way that he was ahead of his time. Some sports writers slammed him early on saying that this would never work in professional basketball.

But it did work — and it worked great. If everyone knows he's going to see some playing time, it's a huge incentive not only to practice harder but also to remain very focused at game time, even while sitting on the bench. That strategy also gave us starters a little more rest and helped our team build quality depth. Proof that Hubie was right with this theory can best be seen in this statistic: during our 1975 championship game, we had 10 guys play and only one failed to score in double figures.

Second: Coach Brown believed in the importance of the point differential. A person who doesn't worry about "small stuff" would never even get to this statistic, but Hubie did. The point differential is how many points your team scores per game minus how many points you give up per game. If you average 100 points per game scored and average 100 points per game given up, statistically, you are going to win half your games and lose half your games. Hubie was all about widening this gap. He felt that a team with a five-point differential would be a true contender for a championship. During the 1974-75 season, our differential was seven, a truly big gap in a game where small things can mean so much.

To achieve this differential, Coach Brown made sure that small things were executed on a more regular basis. One example was that he insisted that the ball come through me more often. It wasn't as simple as that, though. Throughout my career, some people have rapped me for having bad hands. Hubie did not believe that, but he did believe that in order for me to catch the ball properly, I needed to be in the best possible position. So, that's what we worked on. During that year, I averaged 16 shots per game versus 15 shots per game the year before. Sounds like small stuff, right? Only one more shot per game. Well, I got better shots, my field-goal percentage shot up nine points, and my scoring average went from 18.7 points to 23.6. That's enough of an improvement to mean the difference in many games.

The season's total results were terrific. I ranked first in the ABA in minutes (3,493), second in rebounding (16.2 rebounds per game), second in field goal percentage (.580), second in blocks (3.1 blocks per game), and sixth in scoring (23.6 points per game). The Kentucky Colonels finished with a 58-26 record, including a 22-3 mark in the last 25 games. We won the title with a 12-3 post-season run. I ranked first in playoff rebounding (17.6 rebounds per game) and was near the top in postseason leaders for scoring, field goal percentage, and blocked shots. I averaged 25 points per game, 21 rebounds per game, and 1.2 blocks per game in our 4-1 series win over Indiana in the ABA Championship. In Game 3's victory, I rang up 41 points and 28 rebounds, and in the Game 5 series clincher, I had 28 points and 31 rebounds.

It gives me great pleasure to publicly thank Coach Brown for helping me to understand the "small stuff" that made me a better player. Stan Albeck, who was Hubie's assistant coach, was also a big part of this year of growth and success.

I have learned, through men like Hubie Brown, that attention to detail is not selective — it's an everywhere, everything, all-the-time way of living. Although Coach Brown concentrated on my offense, he helped my defense by doing something that a lot of players hate — he benched me. Hubie realized that I benefited from quick rests, and he would sit me down for two-and-a-half minute breaks at the end of the first, second, and third quarters. He would then expect me to run hard the entire fourth quarter — which I could because his attention to the small stuff had helped preserve my stamina down the stretch.

When I say we sweated *and sweated* the small stuff, I mean it. Hubie was a real stickler as far as rules and regulations. Plus, he had no problem getting up in a guy's face and yelling until he ran out of breath. A couple times he lit into me so bad, cursing at full volume, that other guys felt bad for me and tried to calm him down. Maurice Lucas actually got benched once for telling Hubie to stop yelling at me. As long as you got the job done, he was easy to get along with, but there's no doubt that he was a tough cookie and would get on you and stay on you until everything was done right.

But you know what? I never minded. I've played for coaches who let everything slide. That's great in one way because the atmosphere is relaxed. With Hubie, it sure wasn't relaxed, but we always felt that there was purpose in his leadership. Some guys make rules just to be big shots. Hubie made rules because they related to winning. Take, for example, his rule about how we should act out on the court around the other team. Apart from maybe shaking hands before the game, Hubie didn't want us talking to the other guys. It was war, and they were the enemy. If you knocked a guy down — leave him on the ground — don't offer him a helping hand. That had nothing to do with sportsmanship nor was it "small stuff" as it may seem. It was yet another way he had of keeping us centered and thinking only about what needed to be done to win.

Even practice was serious business. There was no goofing around and definitely no goofing off. Horse around or laugh a little too loud, and Hubie would crack down on you. You were expected to be on time. If you weren't, you paid a fine, and you paid a bigger price when Hubie got a hold of you. Even *before* practice started, you didn't just grab a ball and start shooting. Hubie had certain drills that were "pre-practice" drills. No one disobeyed these expectations because Hubie could get very intense, and that's putting it delicately! Yet guys didn't have a problem with any of this. First of all, we accepted his leadership because his knowledge and concepts of the game helped us all. Second, because of the first fact, we became winners.

Coach Brown would go on to a highly successful coaching career in the NBA, but those of us who played with the Kentucky Colonels in the ABA will forever be proud that Hubie has called us "the best team, talent-wise, that I ever coached."

Among the many honors I have been fortunate to receive, there is also a statement Coach Brown made about me that I treasure as much as my 1975 ABA Championship ring. "Artis Gilmore was the best center in ABA history," Coach Brown said. "Artis works hard. He listens and accepts criticism. You're talking about one of the all-time nice guys who ever lived. He was the best, and he was just as nice to the equipment man and the trainer. Never late for anything. He was a different kind of guy." Under the scrutiny and tough love of Coach Hubie Brown, I'm proud to have learned the many small ways of winning big.

No Regrets (maybe)

I've enjoyed my life. I have an amazing wife and wonderful kids. I have friends who truly care about me. For much of my early adulthood, I made a very good living doing what many dream about — playing a damn fun game.

Do I have any regrets about my career in basketball? Maybe. I honestly can't make up my mind on this question. I'll explain.

If I had a dollar for every time I've been described as a "Gentle Giant," I'd have considerably more money than I ever made as a player. I've heard the word "giant" so many times that it's almost meaningless to me. When I was younger, my skin was a bit thinner. I know people mean well when they use that particular word, but it's always struck me as interesting that few people think twice about calling a tall guy a "giant." Hardly any of those folks would call an overweight guy a "giant," at least not to his face. I know it doesn't seem like a major issue, and compared to racially motivated slurs and ignorant remarks about physical attributes, it is indeed next to nothing. I bring it up mostly because of how, in my case, the word "giant" has always been linked with the word "gentle."

In most of the world, gentleness is considered a strength. In professional sports, it gets more complicated. The NBA itself — a pretty good authority — describes me on its website this way:

> *"Artis Gilmore's low-key personality and unpretentious playing style certainly didn't generate the hype that illuminated many other star centers of his day. But when he went up for a rebound or to block a shot, everybody knew who he was. Gilmore was perceived as a gentle giant but was fierce in the post. Regarded as one of the strongest men ever to play professional basketball, Gilmore was one of the league's most intimidating centers during the 1970s and 1980s. Most players knew better than to bring the ball to the hoop when the 7-2 Gilmore was in the middle."*

The paragraph above symbolizes a frequently held perception of my career in that, on one hand, my strength and fierceness down low were recognized and accepted. In the same breath, though, there is sometimes the suggestion, present in words like "low-key," "unpretentious," and "gentle," that everything would have been better if I were somehow more aggressive, loud, and downright mean.

Sometimes, I wonder if maybe that is true. People sometimes questioned why I wasn't more aggressive and willing to fight. Many people said I was the strongest player in the league after Wilt Chamberlain retired. Former ABA player George McGinnis once said, "Guys take advantage of his personality and push him around knowing that he won't push back. Maybe if he had a few fights and knocked people around it would be a different story." Peter Carry of *Sports Illustrated* went so far as to suggest "Artis Gilmore is perhaps too much of a gentleman to play in the ABA."

With all due respect to McGinnis and Carry, I think I did all right.

Still, if I had broken a few wrists every month by dunking when I knew I could hurt a guy, maybe the intimidation factor would have resulted in a few more wins. Maybe if I had felt comfortable being vocal with the media, I would be perceived as being more passionate about the game and the level of leadership it requires.

At the same time, I invite younger readers to study the court demeanor of someone like Tim Duncan — a man who felt no need for the cameras — or to hurt or embarrass his opponents on the floor. He came to work well prepared and proceeded to do his job night after night, healthy or hurt, sometimes without changing the expression on his face for weeks. I understand that type of basketball. Is there any reason to believe Tim would've been more effective if he sucker-punched somebody every so often? Of course not. He was content, as he should be, reading about how he scored a "quiet" 35 points to go with his "quiet" 15 rebounds. Quiet points count just as much as noisy points, but they have the advantage of sometimes going unnoticed by the guys you use them to "quietly" beat.

I also invite older fans of the game to recall that the phrase "gentle giant" was used as a subtle slam against Wilt Chamberlain. People said he was too nice, that he didn't have a killer instinct. To those people, I will pass along a reminder that Bill Russell himself said that Chamberlain could do anything he wanted on the court pretty much any time he wanted to do it — but that as a true professional who respected the game, the most important thing for Chamberlain was to enjoy every aspect of the game, to experience basketball in its entirety.

As a player I wanted to be like that and thought of by my peers in that way, too. If it meant taking someone's legs out or head off, it didn't make sense to me.

The men I played against had livelihoods on the floor and lives off it. So did I. On the floor, I wanted to be competitive and dominant, but I wanted to leave the game there, as well.

In one sense, it would have been easy to be an "ungentle giant." Remember that when I played, the league had not adopted tough, anti-fighting rules yet. There was even something called a "punching foul." What passed for a run-of-the-mill foul in my days will now get a player tossed from the game, probably suspended, and certainly fined.

In another sense, I would like to think that my desire to win by using whatever talent I had, rather than using my strength to hurt others in the pursuit of victory, highlights another reality of ball playing in my day. Because there were no hard and fast rules limiting violence — there are even stories of referees throwing punches with players and fans — it was really totally up to the players themselves to make sure the game was basketball and not brawling.

It concerns me that sometimes sports fans equate athletic aggressiveness with the need to harm others. As a partial result of this misconception, we see horrible things occur during sporting events for young people. Little League fathers attack each other. Officials are injured, sometimes even killed. And, worst of all, adults physically abuse children in a tragic belief that by doing so they will make kids better athletes.

Let's not forget that most of the NBA's current rules against fighting, especially those prohibiting players from leaving the bench to join in a fight, grew out of a terrifying incident on December 9, 1977, when Rudy Tomjanovich of the Houston Rockets was almost killed by a punch thrown by Los Angeles Laker Kermit Washington.

This incident has been written about extensively, and there is still plenty of debate about how it happened, why it happened, who started it — and on and on. Books have been published, and documentary films have been made about this one moment in basketball history, so you can easily come to your own conclusions. I will ask you, however, to consider this. Although Rudy eventually recovered, his game was never the same. Kermit, after being fined $10,000 and suspended for 60 days without pay, played for several teams until he retired in 1982 but was for all practical purposes an outcast who was shunned by many people. What was sad about this is that Kermit was a hard-working man and a self-made player who built his strength and was dedicated to hustle as a way of overcoming other limitations, especially on the offensive side of the game. He succeeded in building for himself a highly positive reputation as a guy who focused on his strengths while always working to improve his weaknesses.

Then, in one unfortunate second, he became known — perhaps both fairly and unfairly — not as an admirably aggressive basketball player but as a man of violence. To those who love the sport, I hold this out as an example of the true difference between being 100 percent competitive and being 1 percent accepting of the opinion that anything goes as long as you win.

I know that professional sports come with a lot of "what if?" questions attached. I'll always wonder if there might have been a few more wins if I had done this or hadn't done that or had been a little more this way and a little less that. Sometimes I even wonder about how my career would've turned out if I played in the NBA the whole time. But those are head games that can never be resolved. What can be stated in factual terms are actual performance statistics.

I am proud of the fact that my combined ABA/NBA shot blocking record is 3,178, fourth highest in the history of professional basketball. Rebounding? 16,330, fifth highest in pro history. I also appeared in 670 consecutive ABA/NBA games. I hope you know by this point in the book that I have tried all my life to avoid being seen as someone who brags. I mention these accomplishments because any good basketball fan will recognize that, although it may help to be a "giant" when trying to block shots, get boards, or play through pain, these three particular categories of statistics reflect parts of the game where being "gentle" does little good. Never mistake a quiet person for a soft person. The numbers speak for themselves.

Numbers are secondary in importance to something less concrete but more enduring: earning the respect of those whom we respect. I'll conclude this chapter with a short story involving a player who has my lifelong admiration.

If you go onto Google and run an internet search using the words: "Julius + Erving + Artis + Gilmore," you'll very quickly find detailed accounts of how the famous Doctor J dunked over yours truly in such-and-such a game in such-and-such a year. I think that every fan over the age of 50 seems to remember Doc slamming one down right in front of my face. And you know what? He probably did. And you know what else? I belong to a big club because Doc jammed on almost everyone at some time or another.

It's interesting that such stories seem to be repeated more when it's the "giant" that loses. Chamberlain's famous line was "No one loves Goliath." Well, Chamberlain enjoyed being dramatic, and that's not what I'm getting at here.

My point can better be underscored by using the Slam Dunk competition as an example. The Slam Dunk became a celebrated show in 1976 when the ABA held the first one at halftime of the All-Star Game in Denver. That contest featured a battle between two of the top dunkers of all-time — David Thompson and Julius Erving. George Gervin, Larry Kenon, and I rounded out the field. For those of you who have followed this competition throughout the years, you'll notice that the shorter the player, the more spectacular the dunk seems and the more points that particular contestant will score. It's obvious that a tall guy should be able to dunk more easily, therefore, when he does, it's not quite as exciting. Anyway — that's the excuse I'll use for explaining the many stories of Dr. J dunking on me.

One story that has had much less coverage is one that Doc himself has told about me. According to Doc: "I remember one day I had an early dunk in a game against Artis Gilmore. And he grabbed 40 rebounds that night. And they were like: 'Why did you wake him up?' I was like: 'Well, my bad. I didn't realize that was going to happen.'"

Honestly, I don't remember the night or the 40 boards, but if Doctor J says so, I'm completely happy to know that the giant was not so gentle with him that time around!

Oh — back to the first Slam Dunk contest. Doc won.

*Artis Gilmore
with the
San Antonio Spurs.*

*Artis with
teammates in the
San Antonio Spurs
locker room.*

*Artis Gilmore with
the Boston Celtics.*

Arimo Bologna team photo, 1988-89

Artis Gilmore guarded by Bob McAdoo, 1988-89 season with Bologna Arimo (Italian League).

Artis dunks the basketball playing for Arimo Bologna, 1988-89.

Artis Gilmore with his Italian teammates at the Wailing Wall, Jerusalem, January 1989.

Advantage International presents Kareem Abdul-Jabbar and The Traveling Daedals, Australia and Taiwan, 1989. Front row, l-r: Kyle Macy, Chris Johnson, Ennis Whatley, Norris Coleman, George Gervin Jr., and Tom George. Back row: Johnny Moore, Bob McAdoo, Kareem Abdul-Jabbar, Paul Westhead, Marques Johnson, George Gervin, Dudley Bradley, Artis Gilmore, and Dwayne McLain.

Artis Gilmore with the Belden All Stars kids basketball team in an infomercial for Stahlin Enclosures, 2008.

ARTIS GILMORE

CAREER STATS

POINTS 24,941
REBOUNDS 16,330
BLOCKS 3,178

ABA
Rookie
OF THE
YEAR
1972

ABA
MVP
1972

ABA
Champion
1975

ABA
All-Star
5 TIMES

ALL-ABA
1ST **TEAM**
5 TIMES

ABA
ALL-DEFENSIVE
1ST **TEAM**
4 TIMES

ABA
ALL-TIME
TEAM

NBA
All-Star
6 TIMES

| 1971-1976 | 1976-1982 | 1982-1987 | 1987 | 1988 |

Enola Gay and Artis Gilmore, 1973.

Artis and Enola Gay Gilmore's wedding day

Artis Gilmore with wife, Enola Gay Gilmore, on honeymoon in Las Vegas, 1973

103

Artis enjoying some vacation time in the Caribbean.

Artis with his oldest daughter, Shawna Danielle Gilmore, Wekiwa Springs State Park, early 1970s.

Artis was a licensed scuba diver. Here he posed for a photo with a friend at Wekiwa Springs State Park, early 1970s.

Artis diving at Wekiwa Springs State Park, early 1970s.

Artis and wife, Enola Gay Gilmore, on vacation.

Artis golfing

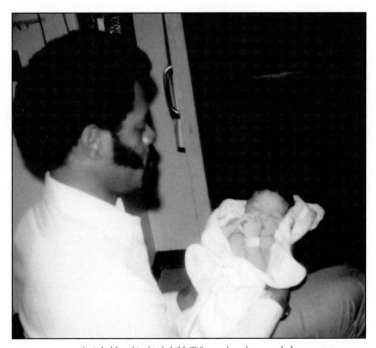

Artis holding his third child, Tifany, when she was a baby.

Artis relaxes on the hood of his new Rolls Royce.

Artis doing the Limbo dance on vacation in the Caribbean.

Left to right: Billy Knight, Artis Gilmore, and Joe C. Meriweather at golf outing, late 1970s.

Artis on a Miami cruise.

Artis enjoying a day of golf.

Artis with wife, Enola Gay Gilmore.

Artis Gilmore early family photo at restaurant (photo taken by Artis), April 16, 1983.

Artis with brother, Patrick Gilmore (left), father Otis Gilmore (right), and children Tifany and Otis James.

Gilmore family outing, early 1980s.

Artis with Enola Gay Gilmore at Taste Disco, Chicago, Illinois, April 24, 1981.

Artis on successful fishing expedition with friend, 1987-88.

Artis' father-in-law, James Maddox (on left) and father, Otis Gilmore (on right), celebrating Otis' 86th Birthday.

Artis enjoying some golf.

Artis Gilmore formal photo, Spring 1990.

Gilmore Family Photo, early 2000s.

Artis enjoying some golf with a friend.

Artis with his wife, Enola, at the Daytona 500.

Artis Gilmore with friends and ABA/NBA legends Rick Barry, David Thompson, and George Gervin.

NYC Masters Basketball

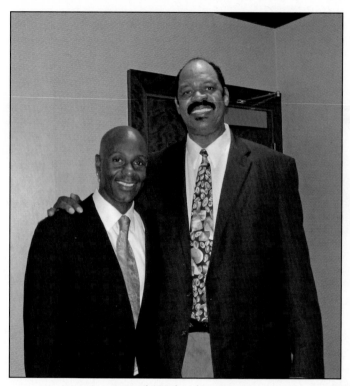

Artis with NFL legend Jerry Rice.

Artis with colleagues at an NBA exhibition in Jacksonville.

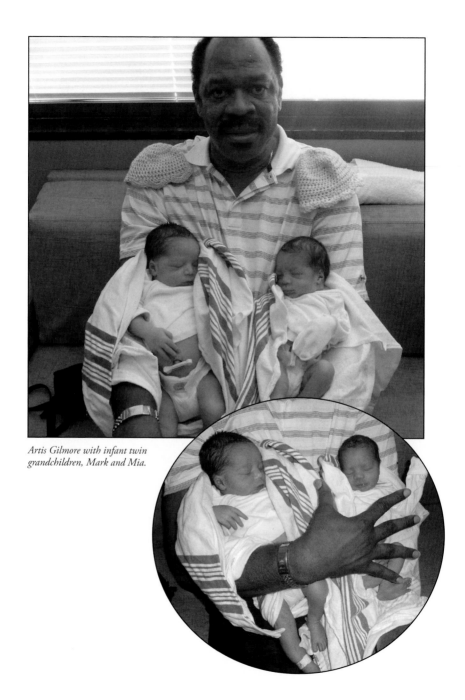

Artis Gilmore with infant twin grandchildren, Mark and Mia.

Artis Gilmore and Enola Gay Gilmore with infant twin grandchildren, Mark and Mia.

Artis with his grandchildren, Mark and Mia, July 2011.

Artis Gilmore, 2011 Hall of Fame Inductee

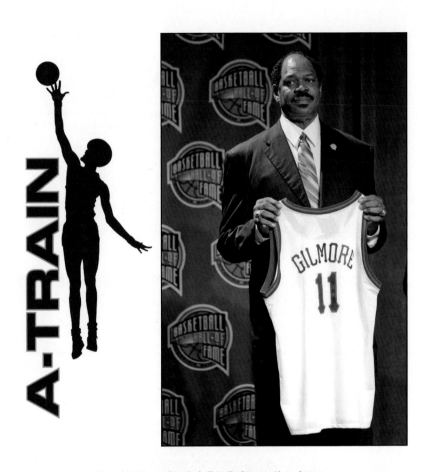

Naismith Memorial Basketball Hall of Fame, Class of 2011.

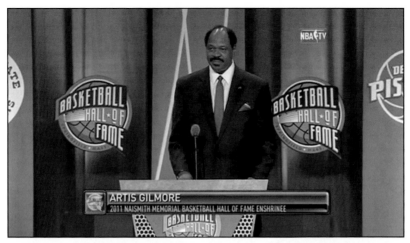

Artis Gilmore, 2011 Naismith Memorial Basketball Hall of Fame Enshrinee.

Artis Gilmore, presented by Julius Erving, giving his acceptance speech at the Naismith Memorial Basketball Hall of Fame, 2011 Enshrinement Weekend.

2011 Naismith Memorial Basketball Hall of Fame Enshrinement: Artis posing with HOF Trophy.

Julius Erving and Artis Gilmore

Artis Gilmore, Rick Barry, Julius Erving, Dan Issel, Rick Kamla, ABA Discussion Panel, Naismith Memorial Basketball Hall of Fame, 2011 Enshrinement Weekend.

Artis Gilmore, Kentucky Athletic Hall of Fame, Class of 2011.

Naismith Memorial Basketball Hall of Fame Reunion Dinner held on Enshrinement Weekend in Springfield, Massachusetts, September 6, 2012. Pictured are Jim Taubenfeld (on the Board of Governors for the Hall of Fame), Artis Gilmore, and Reid Griffith Fontaine.

Naismith Memorial Basketball Hall of Fame Ring Ceremony on Enshrinement Weekend at the Mohegan Sun Resort in Connecticut, September 6, 2013. Pictured are Reid Griffith Fontaine, Moses Malone, Rick Pitino, and Artis Gilmore.

Confucius Never Played
with the Kentucky Colonels

The wise Confucius once said: "Balance is the perfect state of still water. Let that be our model. It remains quiet within and is not disturbed on the surface."

Then again, Confucius never wore the jersey of the Kentucky Colonels in the ABA. If he had, he would have noticed that balance could successfully be achieved even when the waters were boiling and wild with some of the most talented yet freewheeling, eccentric, and sometimes downright crazy ballplayers assembled in one league.

The American Basketball Association. Those who weren't there missed something special. The ABA, in which I began my professional career, was established in 1967 and continued its energetic ride until 1976 when ongoing financial problems and the lack of a national television contract led to a merger with the National Basketball Association. During that time, plenty of exciting and unusual things happened.

George Gervin, an ABA and later NBA great, referred to the NBA in those days as "The Slow Man's League." ABA ball was a more wide-open, offensive-minded style of playing than what one typically saw in the NBA at that time. The ABA was run-and-gun ball at its best. We had the three-point shot, and the NBA did not. That meant an added thrill to the game because we had no shortage of guys itching to throw up long-range bombs. Because of the three-pointer, however, defenses were pulled out closer to the perimeter, which had the effect of opening the lane for guys who loved to slash, drive, and dunk. In this respect, the ABA showed an early resemblance to modern basketball, and as a result, flashy and highly individualistic players emerged into the spotlight.

The ABA was the domain of characters like Marvin "Bad News" Barnes, known for his scoring on the court, as well as for pranking his teammates by waving a nine-millimeter gun at them in the locker room. The gun was empty, but knowing Marvin, no one who dove under the closest bench was taking a chance. Marvin typically stoked up on a pregame meal of nachos and cheese, hot dogs, hamburgers, and Twinkies. Once, after scoring 48 points in a game (obviously having rarely given up the ball once he laid his hands on it), Marvin was overheard telling a reporter that his teammates were selfish ballplayers for not passing to him enough for him to score an even 50 points.

Then there was James "Fly" Williams, who had gotten thirsty during a game and actually dribbled off the court to the nearest fountain for a drink of water. He was also willing to protest what he felt to be a bad call by simply lying down flat in the middle of the court.

Other unique personalities included Maurice "Toothpick" McHartley, who actually played with a toothpick in his mouth, and Bob Netolicky, who, at one time, had a pet lion that slept in his bathtub. There were also some tough characters that lived to play all out. One of the innovative rules of the ABA was that you couldn't foul out of a game. You can imagine how popular that was with guys who naturally liked to club others on the head. One such player was Wendell Ladner, who had a long pedigree as an enforcer. Rumor was Wendell had managed to foul out of a high school game in just 90 seconds!

The ultimate ABA "badass," however, was John Brisker of the Pittsburgh Condors. John liked to fight so much that other teams actually had a cash bounty payable to anyone who could take him physically out of the game — by any means available. Even his own teammates feared John's intensity, and at least one practice was called off when an intersquad fight caused Brisker and his opponent of the moment to run to the locker room for their guns. Real guns.

John eventually made the transition to the NBA with the Seattle SuperSonics but made an enemy of Coach Bill Russell and was soon out of the league. John's family claims that he was invited to Uganda by then-dictator Idi Amin, who was a great basketball fan. John went but disappeared forever. He was declared legally dead in 1985.

This was also the era of the fierce Afro hairstyle. Guys in the ABA even earned nicknames because of the new looks on their heads. Billy Knight, who played for the Indiana Pacers, was called TWA, which stood for Teeny-Weeney-Afro because he couldn't grow much of one. A debate continues until today as to whether Darnell Hillman or I had the largest 'Fro. The website www.rememberetheaba.com claims Darnell is the "runaway winner in the coveted *'Biggest ABA Afro Award at the 1977 ABA Reunion.'*" Maybe so. I tend to believe that because Darnell is a mere 6' 9" tall, it is simply more difficult to gauge from floor level what was the superiority of my hair versus his! Then again, judges might be influenced by the fact that Darnell has still managed to keep a bit more of his hair than I have!

The ABA was also famous — or infamous — for its stunts to attract public attention. The NBA, because of its relative wealth, was able to fund a variety of publicity events, advertising, and fan-based activities. The ABA needed to be more creative … or downright weird. The Indiana Pacers featured a cow-milking contest during one halftime. Remember in the movie *Semi-Pro* when Jackie Moon gets desperate and wrestles a bear? That's not just Hollywood. The Pacers once brought in a wrestling bear named Victor.

My own Kentucky Colonels were not above a bit of Barnum and Bailey theatrics. A few years before I joined the club, the Colonels signed Penny Ann Early, who became the first woman to play in any men's professional basketball league. At 110 pounds and 5' 3", Penny was not warmly received by Coach Gene Rhodes. Nevertheless, management insisted that Penny stay on the roster, which she did until November 28, 1968, when, wearing a miniskirt and sweater with the No. 3, she checked into a game against the Los Angeles Stars. She in-bounded the ball to a teammate, who immediately called timeout. Penny was taken out of the game. The crowd gave her a standing ovation.

In the ABA, we used a colorful red, white, and blue ball, the brainchild of former NBA legend George Mikan, who had become the ABA's first commissioner. The ball created a hypnotic pattern as it turned. Many shooters claimed it helped their technique, but at the very least it was much more visually interesting than the NBA's tired, old, and brown basketball.

In other stylistic ways we felt that we made the NBA guys look a bit — well — boring. They were like big corporation workers with acceptable, groupthink looks. We liked being flashy — even off the court. The ABA was individualistic. We wore bell-bottoms and platform shoes. *Sports Illustrated* called us "The Funkadelic League." They may not have intended that as a compliment, but we took it as one.

We lived to run and dunk. If we could do a 360 before dunking, you bet we'd do it. Our shooters thrived outside the three-point line, an innovation of the ABA that would one day be adopted by the NBA as a player and crowd-pleaser. It is not hard to see how some of these early ABA styles influenced the NBA game in ways that have lasted throughout time and are even quite prominent in the modern era.

In addition to the extreme personalities that made the ABA interesting, bear in mind that some of the world's best basketball talent also played in that league. The NBA certainly tried to make fans believe that there was no comparison in skill levels, but consider the following:

- ABA teams had the winning edge over NBA teams in interleague exhibition games 79 to 76.
- 63 out of a total of 84 ABA players went into the NBA with the 1976 merger, four of whom were on the NBA's top 10 scorers list for that season (George Gervin, David Thompson, Billy Knight, Dan Issel). Don Buse led the entire NBA in assists and steals. Moses Malone and I were third and fourth in league rebounding. My former Colonels teammate, Caldwell Jones, and I were in the top five for blocked shots.
- Half of the NBA Finals starters during 1976-77 were former ABA players, as were nearly half of that year's All-Star team.
- Of the ABA teams merged into the NBA, Denver won the Midwest Division with a 50-32 record, which was the league's second best for that season. Tom Nissalke, a former ABA coach, won NBA Coach of the Year for leading Houston to a divisional championship, and five other ex-ABA coaches took over NBA benches: Hubie Brown in Atlanta; Levin Loughery, Nets; Slick Leonard, Indiana; Doug Moe, San Antonio; Larry Brown, Denver.

The Kentucky Colonels were part of the ABA for all of its nine years and were the winningest franchise in the league's history. For all but the first season, the Colonels played out of Freedom Hall in Louisville, Kentucky.

During their first four years, the Colonels were average at best, with a regular season record of 167-157 and 21-22 in the playoffs. They were, however, able to gain a loyal fan base, due in part to the presence of two Kentucky players: Louie Dampier, who had played with the Kentucky Wildcats, and Darel Carrier, who had starred at Western Kentucky University. Louie played his entire ABA career with the Colonels, and Darel was with the team for five seasons. Both guys were long-range shooters, and the three-point shot was just what they needed to showcase their talents. Louie has the distinction of having scored the most points and made the most assists in the history of the ABA — a truly unusual combination of statistical accomplishments.

Things began picking up for the Colonels during the 1970-71 season when University of Kentucky All-American Dan Issel signed with the team. I played against Dan in the NCAA tournament the year before and knew how great of a player he was. It was no surprise to me when he led the ABA that year, as a rookie, with 29.9 points per game. Despite their significant offensive weapons, however, the Colonels really didn't get rolling during the regular season and barely broke a .500 average. There was also an unsettled atmosphere in management as the team went through three coaches during the season, starting with Gene Rhodes, then moving on to Alex Groza, and finally settling on Frank Ramsey. At playoff time, the Colonels really took off and made it all the way to the ABA title matchup against the Utah Stars. It was a hard-fought, back-and-forth series. In Game 7, despite 41 points from Dan Issel, the Stars pulled out a 131-121 victory, and the Colonels went home to figure out what they needed to do to win it all.

Their first decision was to draft me. My college career at Jacksonville had ended the prior season with a first-round loss in the 1970-71 NCAA tournament against Western Kentucky 74-72. But I averaged 22 points per game, 23 rebounds, and blocked everything at the rim, which was enough to make the pros regard me as the best available center in the 1971 draft. Physically, I had reached my full height of 7' 2," weighing 240 pounds with 27-inch thighs and a 32-inch waist.

In the NBA draft that year, Cleveland had the first pick, but it was actually Chicago that picked me and extended me an offer. Why did I choose the Kentucky Colonels over Chicago? There were essentially two reasons. First, my agent at the time was a young attorney, Herb Rudoy, who continues to represent professional basketball players. At that time he was fairly new to the business, and I was completely new. I was 22 years old, and I had very little exposure to the world outside my corner of Florida. When I went to Louisville to finalize my contract with the Colonels, they bought me a tie, the first I remember owning. That's how little I had been out and about. I was very uncomfortable doing public appearances. I was concerned that being shy would come across as being arrogant or unpleasant. In short, I was depending on professional representation to guide me. Would I have made a different decision had I been older and wiser? Maybe.

But then again, there was a second factor: financial security. Having grown up poor, it was important to me that whatever happened, I would be able to support my family and myself for the long haul. I had a very young attorney, and I had what I thought was a very good support group in Jacksonville. They basically advised me that the ABA was a great opportunity to do some things right away for my family, especially for my mother and father. That was the prize for me because they were certainly very special people in my life. When it came time to sign a contract, I wanted to make sure that I could give something back to my parents. That was always the overriding factor.

It just so happened that my personal motivations in that regard fit in, like a jigsaw puzzle piece, with the way the ABA tended to do business — and certainly the way they attracted star players. Most ABA teams simply did not have deep pockets. Yet, in competing with the NBA for top-quality talent, ABA management realized that the only way they could win was to throw enough money at players. Their solution to this challenge was to offer large dollar contracts but spread out over a number of years. They also came up with what became known as the Dolgoff Plan, named for Ralph Dolgoff, an accountant for the ABA. This was an annuity program featuring a deferred compensation arrangement in which a designated portion of a player's salary would be paid, for a specified period, into some type of mutual or growth fund. After a certain number of years, the plan would start to pay out. These methodologies enabled ABA teams to offer huge, superficially impressive contracts.

It also exaggerated contract offers for public relations benefits. One reason was to keep the NBA off balance. Another reason had to do with the fact that all ABA teams could make sealed bids for players they wanted. The Colonels leaked word that they were willing to pay $3 million for me. That scared off other teams.

Ultimately, the Colonels won their ABA bid, and I accepted a $1.5 million deal, payable at $150,000 over 10 years, plus a $50,000 bonus, and a Dolgoff Plan that paid me $40,000 per year for 20 years beginning in 1981. That was a large contract at the time, and because it covered many years, it also offered me a sense of security that was so important.

Shortly after I became part of the team, the Colonels hired Joe Mullaney as coach to replace Frank Ramsey, who had resigned. It was a great rookie year. The Colonels achieved a regular season record of 68-16, which was incredible. I didn't miss even 1 of the 84 games and was proud to win the ABA's Rookie of the Year and the ABA MVP awards by averaging 23.8 points and 17.8 rebounds per game. The fact that this was also the rookie year of Julius Erving, playing for the Virginia Squires, is a source of professional pride for me. During the season, I was able to improve my game in all respects, but because of Coach Mullaney's emphasis on using me as a defensive weapon, I was able to earn the respect of the great offensive player, Rick Barry, who said I was the greatest shot blocker he had ever seen because of my agility and quick ability to jump outside the paint to block the ball. Rick also noted that referees called many goaltending charges on me simply because no one had ever before seen a player block a shot from 5 or 10 feet away. Their assumption was that the ball had to have been on its downward trajectory. But let me now revise something I just said. It was a great rookie year ... except for one thing. Rick Barry's New York Nets beat us in the first round of the playoffs. Back to the drawing board.

The next season, 1972-73, we won 56 out of 84 regular-season games. Another great showing. That year the playoffs went a bit better with us knocking off Julius Erving and the Virginia Squires four games to one, then the Carolina Cougars with now Hall-of-Famer Billy Cunningham in Game 7. In the ABA championship, we again went a full seven games against the Indiana Pacers and George McGinnis but came up short on our home floor 88-81.

This was getting frustrating. Our fans and the basketball world had begun to doubt our ability to get the job done, despite having all the offensive and defensive weapons to do so.

Although 1973-74 would not be the season to answer our critics, other dynamics occurred that laid the foundation for future success. In July of 1973, the club almost moved to Cincinnati, but Ellie and John Y. Brown, Jr., owners of Kentucky Fried Chicken, purchased majority ownership of the franchise. Ellie, a very innovative businessperson, created for the organization an all-female board of directors. Management efforts in promoting the club doubled our attendance that year. The Browns also hired Babe McCarthy as our new coach. Babe was known by his nickname "Magnolia Mouth" because of his heavy Mississippi drawl. He was also famous for his "Babe-isms," which were usually down-home country expressions such as "My old pappy used to tell me the sun don't shine on the same dog's butt every day."

Well, the sun still wasn't shining on us yet!

Despite going 53-31 in the regular season and a sweep over the Carolina Cougars in round one of the playoffs, Doctor J and the New York Nets busted our backs and our spirits and put us out of the playoffs four games to none. This meant the end of Babe McCarthy as our coach, but it also meant the beginning of Hubie Brown as our new coach. 1974-75 would be our season.

Coach Brown (no relation to Ellie and John Y. Brown) had been winning respect for his hard work as an assistant coach under Larry Costello in Milwaukee with the NBA's Bucks. Shortly after taking over leadership of the Colonels, he brought in Stan Albeck as his assistant. They had worked together before, and Stan had also served as Wilt Chamberlain's assistant during Chamberlain's little-remembered stint as coach of the ABA's San Diego Conquistadors. Hubie and upper management also set about to infuse the club with new talent and brought in five new players: Marv Roberts, Wil Jones, Ted "The Hound" McClain, Bird Averitt, and Gene Littles. Dan Issel, Louie Dampier, Jim Bradley, Ron "the Plumber" Thomas, and I rounded out the team.

Earlier, I wrote in some detail about Coach Hubie Brown but would now like to underscore why he was such an important key to our success in 1975. Coach Brown understood balance.

Having worked with Kareem Abdul-Jabbar in Milwaukee, he knew how to guide big men into being offensive weapons. Although I had been very consistent in my offensive contributions, my points per game rose about five points under Hubie that year (23.6 points per game in the regular season and 24.1 in the playoffs).

Coach Brown matched my inside offensive and defensive presence with the tremendous outside scoring power of Dan Issel and Louie Dampier. On defense, Wil Jones was a guy who could and did give the greats like Julius Erving trouble on the court. Coach would use Wil and Marv Roberts as a small forward combination. He split their time, and regardless of who was on the floor, we maintained the standards of performance we needed. Although we ran no set plays for Wil and Marv, those two guys combined for nearly 20 points per game. It was similar to Pembrook Burrows and Greg Nelson back at JU.

In addition to Wil's outstanding defense, Teddy McClain and Gene Littles were both world-class defenders. Bird Averitt contributed speed. That translated into an ability to move the ball up and down the court faster than the opposition. Ron Thomas filled the very important role of enforcer. In those days, more than now, every team had one guy whose main role in basketball was to bruise the opposition and protect his own team's stars. We also had a young forward named Jim Bradley, who had a ton of talent but became best known for the number of fines charged against him by the coaching staff for being late to practices and games. We figured that the team's postseason party was paid for mostly by Jim's violations.

As you can see from this simple profile of the team, our collective personality was a rare and productive balance between offense and defense. Our championship year featured a regular season that actually did not go so well at first. For most of it, we trailed the New York Nets in the Eastern Division but then went on a rampage and won the tiebreaker. At 58-26, we then beat the Nets 108-99 in a special one-game divisional tiebreaker.

Our first two rounds in the playoffs went pretty smoothly as we beat the Memphis Sounds and then the Spirits of St. Louis, both four games to one. We then had the opportunity for revenge in the title game against the Indiana Pacers, who had eliminated us in 1973. In Game 1, we crushed them 120-94. In Game 2, I scored with three seconds to go to put us ahead by two. But then the Pacers' Billy Keller crushed us with a three-pointer at the buzzer. Unfortunately for Indiana, the officials decided that his bucket came a split second too late, and we were given the game. This broke their spirit, and we knew the championship would be ours. Though we took Game 3, we lost Game 4 in Indiana but captured the series at home in Game 5 by a score of 110-105. I scored 28 points and collected 31 rebounds against George McGinnis and was fortunate enough to be awarded the ABA Playoff MVP award.

After our 1974-75 title, Coach Brown added the word "pressure" to our championship rings as a reminder to all of us that our victories were made possible by our ability to perform when the lights were brightest.

Although I have never been one to argue with Hubie Brown, I may have chosen the word "balance" instead. Our ability to win despite pressure was made possible by balance both on and off the court. Hubie himself was at the heart of our balance. His motto, from day one, was:

TEAM:

Together
Everyone
Accomplishes
More!

... and we did.

Balance was the reason why Hubie was able to use, during almost every game, all 10 guys he had on the team. Every eight minutes during the first three quarters, he would substitute in new players. He did this whether we were winning, losing, or tied. Everyone knew when he would be going in or coming out of the game. During the fourth quarter Hubie would take over full command and substituting would match the needs of the individual contest. He was able to manage the team because we had so many combinations of interchangeable parts, all of which met the need for maintaining size, speed, offensive firepower, rebounding, and stubborn defense.

The result of balance, in a team sport like basketball, is not only that you can achieve mastery over the style of ball played by your own team but also that you can adjust to whatever style of basketball is brought onto the court by the opposing team. Remember: the greats create. In our case, if the other guys wanted to run, we had the legs to run. If they wanted to play a half-court game, we could shut them down on one end and run them off on the other. We had the long arms and quick feet to trap and to press on defense, in addition to the quickness and good passing to escape from similar defensive tactics when used against us.

As I've said before, it is not necessary for the individuals on a team to personally like each other in order to be professionally successful. It does, however, make balance easier to achieve and basketball in general more enjoyable. Our championship Kentucky Colonels team was close off the court. We had a few advantages that other teams didn't have. For example, we flew to most of our games in a corporate Gulfstream 1 prop-jet — something that few other teams benefited from. We traveled comfortably, and it kept us better rested. We also socialized away from basketball, whether on the golf course or at parties. I believe that friendship away from the gym gave us an even stronger feeling of team camaraderie when facing our opponents. We knew who we were and what we could do.

The concept of balance and the power of achieving balance go beyond talent itself. In the game of basketball, as it's played today, the effort to find five-man team balance too often gives way to isolation-style ball playing where one superstar is matched up against another, mano a mano. The rest of the players on both teams step back and watch the big guns do their thing. On defense, a blocked shot that smashes the ball into the stands might excite the crowd and embarrass the poor guy who attempted the shot, but it is a ridiculous example of individual versus team play. The great shot blocker, Bill Russell, repeatedly made the point that a good shot blocker doesn't worry about looking like a big man. He worries about blocking a shot skillfully so the ball stays in play and his team has a chance of getting the ball and scoring on a fast transition.

A lot of focus today is on the glory of individual play and individual achievements, which is exactly why the teams with the most individual talent do not necessarily always win. The best (but most painful to watch) example of this has been the failures of U.S. Olympic and FIBA world basketball teams to win the gold medal a little more than a decade ago. You could argue they didn't have adequate time to work together, and that may be a partial excuse. The deeper reason seems to be, however, that "American" style basketball, including the NBA, has glorified individual achievements to such an extent that in international competitions, talent-loaded U.S. teams filled with the best professional athletes on the planet cannot always win against teams that truly play as teams: moving the ball, passing the ball, creating opportunities for each other.

Those who watched the 2006 FIBA World Championship might remember how difficult it was for fans of the U.S. squad to watch Greece run fundamental play after fundamental play. Were they flashy? No. In fact, they were predictable but were executed so well that they could not be stopped. Was the Greek team more talented than the U.S. man-for-man? No. But they had team balance, and no one player — or two — or three, no matter how gifted, has much of a chance against the power of balance.

I am pleased that Team USA has fixed some of these problems and won its third straight gold medal. When our teams strike the balance of individual talent and team play, we're certainly hard to beat.

A lot of talented teams never find this balance, and that is why our 1974-75 Kentucky Colonels team was so exceptional. True, we were guided by the firm hand, basketball intelligence, and loud yelling of Coach Hubie Brown, but we were a bunch of young guys playing in what, at its basic level, was a league filled with players who excelled at being individualists. Therein, however, is a truth that many people miss about basketball. Working to become a balanced team does not limit the ability of a player to express individualism — it enhances it by making more opportunities possible.

Let me give you a prime example. As great as he was, Michael Jordan did not achieve his true superstardom until he bought in (even if a bit begrudgingly) to the concept of the Triangle Offense as defined by coaches Tex Winter and Phil Jackson. On the surface level, having to conform to a plan may have seemed to limit Michael's individual flexibility. In reality, and deeply below the surface of the game, it actually involved his entire team in the flow of the game, thereby creating more opportunities for Michael and every other man on the squad. A fistful of championship rings proved that to be true.

The incredible thing about basketball is that the combination of possibilities is literally endless. Take a step left and endless possibilities for your next move become available to you. Take a step right and another, but very different, set of endless possibilities becomes available. Multiply that by the steps and endless possibilities created by nine other guys. Then you can easily see that the only way that individualism can survive and thrive in such an environment is by accepting the fact that fundamental knowledge of the game leads to an appreciation of discipline, which in turn enables an individual to make choices that effectively focus the strengths of his entire team, which, in turn, leads to balance, which, in turn, is the best opportunity for victory.

Confucius may have understood balance in nature, but the 1975 Kentucky Colonels understood balance on the basketball court.

Durability, Discipline, and Luck

I played professional basketball for 17 years. That's a long time. Especially when you realize that the average career for a professional basketball player is slightly less than four years.

During that time, I played in 670 consecutive games in one stretch, never missing an ABA game, and appeared in 250 consecutive games with the Chicago Bulls until I badly damaged my knee in the fourth game of the 1979-80 season. At that time, I had not missed a game since high school when I had the measles. Even then, I would have played if they had let me. Eager to get back into action with the Bulls, I rushed my rehab, which ended up delaying my intended return. When I was able to play again, I put in another 212 straight games.

During my career, I played with the flu many times, with a cast on my ankle, with badly pulled hamstrings, with dozens of stitches, scores of concussions, and with a badly scratched eyeball ... to name a few bumps and bruises. Am I proud of this? Darn right I am!

I've heard the first step to success is simply showing up. I believe that. I also believe that showing up is not simple. I wanted my reputation to ride on being seen as a man who would do his job, come hell or high water. My work ethic was, I believe, a key reason why I was able to be an ABA or an NBA All-Star for 11 of the 17 years I played, including my last selection at the age of 36 — a modern dinosaur by the standards of professional sports.

I'm not alone among durable big men. My longtime rival, Kareem Abdul-Jabbar, put in 20 bruising years in the league. Robert "Chief" Parish, my one-time teammate, beat Kareem by one year. Dikembe Mutombo Mpolondo Mukamba Jean-Jacques Wamutombo, more commonly known as Dikembe Mutombo, began his long professional career during the 1991-92 season and retired in 2009. Dikembe's official biography lists his year of birth as 1966, but people have openly speculated that Dikembe may in fact be anywhere between the age of 41 and 85! Just kidding, Dikembe.

I'll be the first to admit that luck has a lot to do with a long career. I suffered only one major injury, despite years in the most physical position in basketball. But luck is further down the list of reasons for true durability.

I have said before that discipline is a key to freedom. I don't necessarily mean discipline in the sense of someone yelling in your face until you do something the way they want it done. Nor does discipline always mean doing without and self-sacrificing. My outlook on discipline begins with the willingness just to put one foot ahead of the other; to show up on time, all of the time; to listen to what others have to say; to watch how others conduct themselves and do their jobs; to rein in reckless behavior; to adjust when necessary; and to practice the craft you have chosen. The "great create," but in order to create, you have to be there.

Some great players hate practice. Bill Russell did not like to practice. Allen Iverson, quite infamously, publicly questioned the importance placed on his need to practice. For most of us, though, whether it's sports or business, practicing is the cornerstone of discipline.

First, it keeps us in good condition. The easiest way to spot an amateur basketball player is to roll a ball out onto the court. The guy who comes in cold, grabs the ball, and starts running around jacking up threes is either a teenager who is perpetually limber or an older fellow who doesn't know any better. Almost everyone who is serious about the game doesn't just jump into the game without first going through a series of stretches, grunts, moans, groans, and various exercises designed to keep the body from seizing up once the actual contest begins.

In my day, weight training was not emphasized in basketball, although some players were really into it. The common wisdom was that becoming muscle-bound would disrupt the fine tuning necessary for proper, effective shooting techniques. Of course, times change and now players focus on building their bodies. Although there is no guarantee that even the strongest, most physically fit athlete won't suffer a career-ending injury through bad luck, it cannot be denied that players can make their own "luck" by being physically prepared.

Being mentally prepared is the other half of the equation. It's interesting to me how much the physical and mental worlds overlap. In basketball, for example, one reason for repeatedly running drills is for physical conditioning. The deeper reason, however, is that repetition of an act eventually imprints a discipline in the human mind that allows a person to do things by intuition. On the basketball court, practicing a play so many times that it makes you sick pays off during games not only when that particular play works — but more often when it doesn't. The freedom of discipline often comes from when what you have planned fails. It is that split second between initial failure and your next action that makes the difference between changing a failure into a success or letting it become a permanent failure. Because both basketball and life present so many options, the person who intuitively knows the best "next move" is the person who stays one step ahead of the competition. That level of intuitiveness, how-ever, typically only comes from the hard work of practicing what you do best and practicing even harder on those things that are your weaknesses.

In the previous chapter, I recounted a pivotal season in my professional life: the ABA championship season of 1974-75, commenting on how balance and discipline went hand in hand in contributing to team victory. Unfortunately, balance is difficult to maintain when many strong forces are out of your control.

The Kentucky Colonels looked ahead to the 1975-76 season with great ex-pectations. We saw no reason why we couldn't repeat as champions. Then things began to change. Our owner John Y. Brown, Jr. traded Dan Issel to the ABA's new franchise, the Baltimore Claws. The rumor has always been that John Y., in an effort to ensure a profit that year, figured he needed to put either Dan or me on the market. The Colonels, despite being ABA champs, were still in the red financially. He decided on Dan, apparently because he felt I would have a longer career and calculated that he could make $500,000 for the "sale."

To add insult to injury, the Claws were a nonviable business and never even took the floor in an actual game. That was bad for Dan but also for John Y., in that the Claws were obviously unable to pay the amount of money they had committed to. Another deal was worked out, and Dan ended up with the Den-ver Nuggets, and Dave Robisch came to the Colonels as part of the arrangement. Additionally, Ted McClain was sold to the New York Nets for $150,000. From a business perspective, John Y. argued that he was only thinking of the financial health of the Colonels franchise. Our fans, however, were almost unanimously unhappy with the loss of both men and thought it odd that they would be sent away so soon after having contributed in a major way to the ABA championship. Attendance dropped to an average of 6,957, down more than 2,000 per game from the year before.

We also acquired from the San Diego Sails' Caldwell Jones, who was an All-Star player, but never seemed to quite fit in, at least in the eyes of management. Caldwell was a center, but because of my presence, he played forward, a position with which he was perhaps not entirely comfortable. He was traded midseason to the Spirits of St. Louis for Maurice Lucas. Maurice was a strong addition to the team, but other trades (Marv Roberts to the Virginia Squires for Jan van Breda Kolff and Johnny Neumann) kept team chemistry unstable through no real fault of the individual players involved. On top of this, the relationship between Hubie Brown and management was in the dumps. We managed to stay competitive throughout the regular season, but too many players had come and gone. We barely squeezed by the Indiana Pacers, winning round one of the playoffs two games to one. We then faced the Denver Nuggets, who had finished first in the regular season. We gave them a run for their money but lost in Game 7, 133-110.

And then life changed. In June 1976, the American Basketball Association and the National Basketball Association merged. Four ABA teams — the Denver Nuggets, New York Nets, San Antonio Spurs, and Indiana Pacers — all joined the NBA and still exist today (with the Nets now specifically in Brooklyn). All other remaining teams, including the Kentucky Colonels, vanished forever from the world of basketball.

The four ABA teams that merged with the NBA each paid $3.2 million for the privilege. Kentucky Colonels owner John Y. elected not to pay the entry fee. He instead negotiated a buyout with the NBA and received $3 million. He later bought, for approximately $1.5 million, what was then the NBA franchise Buffalo Braves. He later made a deal to swap franchises with the owner of the Boston Celtics. John Y., who also became governor of Kentucky in 1979, made out extremely well, but the Kentucky Colonels were no more.

Behind the scenes, the Chicago Bulls also had a motivation in keeping the Colonels out of the NBA. They held first draft rights to me and were coming off a horrible year, so they really wanted me on their team. The Bulls' management, therefore, encouraged the NBA to accept only four ABA teams, thereby contributing to the decision of John Y. Brown to opt out for cash.

As a result, at the age of 26, I was selected in the dispersal draft by the Chicago Bulls. My teammates from the 1975 championship went elsewhere. Following is a short list of key draft picks involving former Colonels:

- Chicago: Artis Gilmore, $1.1 million
- Portland: Maurice Lucas, $300,000
- Buffalo: Bird Averitt, $125,000
- Indiana: Wil Jones, $50,000
- Houston: Ron Thomas, $15,000
- San Antonio: Louie Dampier, $20,000

A big chapter in my life had ended. In my five ABA seasons, I never averaged fewer than 18.7 points or 15.5 rebounds, and I won the league rebounding title four out of five seasons. Other key highlights included:

- ABA championship, Kentucky Colonels, 1975
- ABA Most Valuable Player and Rookie of the Year, 1971-72
- One of seven unanimous selections to the 1997 ABA All-Time Team
- Regular season ABA numbers: 22.3 points and 17.1 rebounds. Play-off averages: 22.0 points and 16.1 rebounds.
- Four-time ABA rebounding champion (1972-74, 1976)
- Two-time ABA field goal percentage champion (1972, 1973)
- Two-time ABA shot blocking champion (1972, 1973)
- 1974 ABA All-Star Game MVP
- 1975 ABA Playoff MVP
- Five-time All-ABA First-Team selection (1972-76)
- Four-time ABA All-Defensive Team selection (1973-76)
- ABA single-season record for the most blocked shots (422)
- ABA regular season single-game record of 40 rebounds (versus New York, February 3, 1974)
- Played in all 420 games during a five-year ABA career.
- Finished in the top 10 in scoring all five seasons.

When I left for Chicago, I felt prepared for anything. I was excited about a new challenge yet a bit sad that the Kentucky Colonels could not have entered the NBA as a team. I will always believe that our 1974-75 squad could have risen to the top of any league. But that is the way of the world.

The way of an individual within that ever-changing world is to put one foot in front of the other, use what you have learned, and do your best to do the job you have chosen. Those who have learned this lesson tend to stay around the longest. With a little luck.

ONE NIGHT IN BOSTON

PART TWO

Remembering.
Being Remembered.

Twenty-one years earlier, on December 22, 1967, I saw my first professional basketball game at the Boston Garden. Now, on June 1, 1988, I was a bit closer to the action but not as close as I'd like to be. Four months earlier, on January 8, 1988, I signed with the Boston Celtics after the Chicago Bulls waived me. My minutes per game had fallen from 43.6 in 1972 to just 11.1 at the end of my career. My view of the famous parquet floor was mostly from the bench. Two days later in Detroit, my career as an NBA basketball player would end.

Did I know this was my last stand? Probably. I know that I didn't want it to be. I know that I felt I had more left in me. Yet the heart usually knows what the head is sometimes slow to admit.

Sure, it had been a good run. Why else, after 1,556 college, ABA, and NBA regular season, All-Star, and playoff games, would I still want it all to continue? Nonetheless, those closing moments in Boston did not define the success of my NBA career — it accrued over several years in the newly merged league, which was only possible due to my experiences from childhood, college, and the ABA. Regardless of when, where, or how my career ended in the NBA, it was those earlier experiences that gave me the tangibles and the intangibles to compete in the NBA and immediately dominate for the Chicago Bulls.

I came to Chicago in 1976, 27 years old, through the dispersal draft, and in a couple years, I earned a seven-year, $4.5 million contract. I wore an ABA championship ring, and I was ready for anything. The challenge was going to be significant. The Bulls were coming off a horrible season in 1975-76, their worst until the turn of the century, with a measly 24 wins. Ed Badger was the coach at first, but soon Jerry Sloan came in, and like Hubie Brown, he was a hard-nosed competitor with endless energy and the ability to motivate every ounce of talent out his players. I had played against the Bulls in exhibition matches during my last two years in the ABA, and although we had beaten Chicago, I knew enough about guys like Norm Van Lier and Bob Love to know that this was a team that was scrappy, willing to hustle, and willing to bang heads.

Norm was our captain, and he commanded the respect of everyone because of his physical and mental strength. Moreover, he was a great people person. Norm and Tom Boerwinkle went out of their way to make me feel welcome and to help me adjust to playing in the NBA. As a team, we did not socialize off the court as much as the Colonels did, but there were no real conflicts either, and once in the gym, everyone seemed focused on working together.

The 1976-77 season started out with a loud thud. We played terribly. After starting 2-1, we lost 13 consecutive games. I was not used to this, but I was even more unprepared for the backlash by fans and the media. As a small-town guy who had just played ball in Kentucky, it was a bit of an adjustment to the big stage of Chicago. I had been touted as the salvation for the team. With me at center, there was no way that the Bulls could lose. The newspapers were all over my case. What's wrong with Gilmore? For the first time ever, I felt the heat of criticism for not carrying an entire team on my back. That was especially uncomfortable because I was shy throughout my career about talking to the press. It wasn't that I didn't want to or that I was anti-media. It just didn't come easily for me. This intensified matters because I know it made me look like I felt that I was selfish or unwilling to face criticism.

By the All-Star break, we were still performing poorly, five or six games out of playoff contention, and far out of the divisional lead. Interestingly, I had a feeling throughout the season, even when we were losing night after night, that we were a good team that just hadn't found itself yet. Time was running out, though, and we had only 27 games in which to make up the big difference.

Then it happened — a surge that took its name from the location of the old Chicago Stadium and became known as "The Miracle On Madison Street." Norm kept us all together on the floor with toughness and leadership that didn't always show up in the box score. Mickey Johnson was outstanding; he wasn't a true power forward, so sometimes he played on the wing. He was aggressive, hard-working, and a really smart player, too. His play down the stretch, and especially in the playoffs, was just incredible. Mickey was from Chicago, so he always gave his best for the hometown crowd. Unfortunately, we never had a chance to experience the true skills of Scott May. He was our small forward but was hurt for three straight years. He had mono as a rookie, then an injury to one knee plagued him the next season. By his third season, he'd injured his other leg. Scott had a very difficult time as a pro, but as the 1976-77 season wore on, he grew stronger and contributed. Wilbur Holland and John Mengelt understood their roles. Both knew where they fit in — Wilbur the starter, John off the bench. Both were great streaky shooters. Wilbur was quick on defense, and John played hard defensively, very much like Jerry Sloan did as a player.

With that core group, we dug ourselves out of our hole, going 20-4 to end the season and qualify for the playoffs versus the Portland Trail Blazers. We had two winning streaks of seven and eight games during that stretch, beating good teams in the process. We met up with Kareem Abdul-Jabbar and the Los Angeles Lakers twice and beat them both times. Just thinking back on our run makes my head spin.

But we weren't thinking about just making the playoffs. We knew we were the hottest team in basketball, and in a short three-game series, we felt like we were the favorites. We all felt we could go all the way.

Against Portland, I would face Bill Walton, a formidable opponent, with a game style very different from my own. As I mentioned earlier, Walton later said I gave him more trouble than anyone he ever played against. He thought Kareem Abdul-Jabbar was a better player than me, but Bill also knew I gave him the biggest headaches because of my overpowering play on both ends of the court.

We dropped Game 1 in Portland 96-83, which immediately put our backs against the wall. Thankfully, Game 2 was home in Chicago, and we knew the place was going to be jam-packed and wild. The city went from being somewhat uninterested in our team for much of that season to going crazy.

The Bulls had started using a spotlight for their pregame introductions. In the stretch run, we were regularly drawing standing-room-only crowds, with people being turned away outside. Imagine the thrill of being introduced in complete darkness, with 18,000 people screaming for you; it was unlike anything I'd experienced before. The crowd was our sixth man. The support and enthusiasm from our fans was unbelievable.

Game 2 was every bit the battle we anticipated. It was a back-and-forth game, tied after the first quarter. At halftime, we had a slim 50-46 lead. Right before the half, there was a little skirmish between Wilbur and Portland's Herm Gilliam. As usual, Portland's Maurice Lucas, my former Colonels teammate, jumped in the middle of it all, and quickly this altercation blew up into a real bare-knuckles fight. Our assistant coach, Gene Tormohlen, was trying to pull Gilliam off Wilbur with his hands around Gilliam's neck when Maurice punched him. This game was the most intense we'd played all season — do or die — and it was getting tenser by the minute. After three quarters, our lead was down to 79-77. Neither team was able to run away with this one.

As expected, the game came down to the last few minutes. It was all tied up at 94, with five or six minutes left, when Portland's Dave Twardzik drove for a layup that I blocked. The fans had been buzzing all night but seemed a little nervous about the outcome — they exploded after the swat. We really broke out on defense after that, and two buckets from Wilbur gave us some breathing room, 98-94.

I sealed the game with a hook shot, my go-to move, over Walton. Lucas fouled me on the play, and I hit the free throw, giving me 27 points, 11 rebounds, and 5 blocks for the game. We ended up winning 107-104 to send the series back to Portland for the third and deciding game.

Afterward, everyone was talking as if I had triumphed over Walton, but that wasn't the case. It was a team effort. Walton had a great game, too. I was able, however, to establish position deep on him early in the game, and with my strength, he was forced to foul me often: He had five fouls in the third quarter, and that hurt Portland. Even without Walton, though, the Blazers kept up with us. That team showed a lot of poise. It's no surprise they went on to win the championship that year after taking Game 3 from us in Portland, 106-98. I ended the season averaging 18.6 points, 13.0 rebounds (fourth in the league), and 2.48 blocked shots (also fourth).

My second season in Chicago brought the first of six inclusions on the NBA All-Star Team, as I posted averages of 22.9 points per game and 13.1 rebounds per game. The Bulls, however, struggled to a 40-42 record and missed the playoffs. I feel obligated, as much as it pains me, to also mention that during this season I also set a record that still stands: 366 turnovers, the most in one NBA season at the time. Please don't repeat that statistic. Just recently, James Harden took this ignominious record from me, and I'm more than okay with that. Thanks, James!

Our 1978-79 season was even more disappointing. My averages were 23.7 points per game, 12.7 rebounds per game, plus a second All-Star appearance, but as a team, we regressed to a 31-51 record and once again couldn't reach the playoffs.

Early in the 1979-80 season, I hurt my knee, and the Bulls were not able to make much headway. During the 1980-81 season, though, we made up some lost ground. I delivered another All-Star season, and we swept the New York Knicks in the opening round of the playoffs. But, in turn, Larry Bird and the Boston Celtics swept us in the Eastern Conference Semifinals.

I would spend one more season in Chicago, making the All-Star team again, but the Bulls again failed to qualify for the postseason. I left Chicago with mixed emotions. On one hand, I feel like I pulled my weight. I was very consistent and delivered night in and night out. In six seasons with the Bulls, I averaged at least 17.8 points and 9.0 rebounds, and I played 82/82 games in five of them.

Though I had still put up solid numbers, I was the focus for what is a never-ending give-and-take in the world of professional sports. "How much can one player be expected to do?" Over the years it has been said that I didn't look mean enough. Or that I didn't use my strength enough. Or that I was too predictable. Too mechanical. One columnist wrote that I had a "6' 2" soul in a 7' 2" body."

All those comments hurt at the time, and frankly, they still do. But I understand that professional sports will always be judged by final outcomes. I also accept — although I'm not sure I necessarily understand — that the expectations of big men in basketball are directly proportional to their size. Critics will try to say that basketball is a team sport, but they often point blame on the most visible individual.

I have always made a personal rule to let fans decide what to believe. I will point out, however, that numbers should speak for themselves. During the 1978-79 season, I nearly matched my ABA high in scoring with a 23.7-point average, placing ninth in the league. In Chicago Bulls history, I rank first in blocked shots (1,029), tenth for games played (482), tenth in minutes played (16,777), seventh in points (9,288), sixth in rebounds (5,342), first in field goal percentage (.587), seventh in field goals made (3,466), fifth in free throws made (2,355), and fourth in free throw attempts (3,307). I led the Bulls in scoring, rebounding, field goal shooting, and blocked shots in three consecutive seasons and four overall (1976-78 and 1981). I led the team in field goal shooting and blocked shots in 1980. I played in the All-Star Game in four of my six seasons with Chicago.

In Chicago I also picked up the nickname that has followed me ever since. "A-Train" was a Chicago transit train, and a local broadcaster once said that I "came down the lane like the A-Train." It stuck. I've got to admit, I like it.

As for Chicago itself and Bulls fans in general — I thought it was a wonderful city to play in. I don't have a championship ring from Chicago, but I still consider myself part of that family, part of the franchise. I adopted the Cubs as my baseball team, and it gave me great joy to see them finally break the curse in 2016!

It has been said (including by Chicago's general manager Rod Thorn in comments to the media) that at the end of the 1981-82 season, I demanded to be traded. That's just not true. Those who know me know that I have never been a person to turn my back when the going gets tough. That was a decision that was made elsewhere, by the powers that be.

Regardless, on July 22, 1982, I was traded to the San Antonio Spurs for Dave Corzine, Mark Olberding, and cash. The Spurs were an ABA team that had transferred to the NBA, and my addition to the club gave us a powerful inside-outside combination with my teammate George "Iceman" Gervin. That season we won a then-franchise record 53 games and made it to the Western Conference Finals, losing to the defending champion Lakers 4-2 in a tough battle against Kareem Abdul-Jabbar, Magic Johnson, and the original Showtime crew.

Stan Albeck was our head coach that year. Stan was Hubie Brown's assistant when we won it all with the Kentucky Colonels in 1975. We had just beaten the Denver Nuggets handily to advance to the conference finals, and we were confident that we could beat the Lakers and compete for the NBA Championship. We split the first two games in Los Angeles, which really gave us a lot of confidence, but then we came back home and lost the next two games to fall behind, 1-3. Everyone figured that we were done at that point, but we were able to win another big game back in Los Angeles. Unfortunately, we were never able to win a game on our home court. The Lakers played great basketball when they needed to, and they were able to advance.

That season I led the league in field goal percentage (.626), while ranking fourth in rebounding (12.0 rebounds per game) and fifth in blocks (2.3 blocks per game). I also personally feel that I defended Kareem better than any other center in the league. I was able to play even the best centers one-on-one, thereby eliminating the need for consistent double teams from my teammates. Later, in interviews, Kareem was kind enough to acknowledge our combat by saying that although he always felt he could outplay anyone, I was an "enormous challenge" because I had the physical skills to counter his every move.

It was also a very special honor to play with George Gervin after so many years of competing against him in both the ABA and NBA. He was such a phenomenal offensive threat. They called him "Iceman" because he was so cool under pressure, and he certainly lived up to the nickname. I'm lucky and grateful to say George and I still maintain a friendship, even all these years after our playing days. I also keep up with other former ABA rivals like Julius Erving and did stay in touch with Moses Malone before he tragically passed away in 2015. He was a tremendous man, and I, along with the rest of the basketball world, will miss him dearly.

Although some in the media thought I might have been too old to contribute to the Spurs at the age of 33, we went on to repeat as division winners in 1982-83, and I returned to the All-Star Game. Over a three-game stretch in March, I compiled 96 points and 35 rebounds. Our 53-29 record was the Spurs' best since the franchise joined the league in 1976. We advanced to the conference finals for the second straight year.

By the mid-1980s, however, the Spurs were a team on the decline. We won between 28 and 41 games per year during my final four years on the team and made the playoffs only twice, losing in the first round both times. Injuries to point guard Johnny Moore and myself left us at 37-45 in 1983-84. Even still, I was able to lead the NBA in field goal percentage (.631) and ranked fifth in blocks (2.1 blocks per game).

I continued playing at a high level into the 1984-85 season. I ranked in the top 10 in field goal percentage (.623; second), blocks (2.1; seventh), and rebounds (10.4 rebounds per game; tenth), but we were knocked out in the first round of the playoffs.

Alas, Father Time showed his eternal strength. Age had begun to take its toll. In 1985-86, I failed to average at least 10 rebounds per game — just the second time in 15 professional seasons, and the other time was in my injury-shortened year. Still, I managed to rank second in field goal percentage (.618) that year and again in 1986-87 (.597). As a team, the Spurs were also in a slow decline and unable to find a championship formula.

Bob McAdoo, who starred with the Lakers during this time, once said: "Artis was with the Spurs when we were at the height of our powers in L.A. Let's face it. Winning a title takes some luck, and Artis didn't get that lucky."

I ended my run with the Spurs with some notable entries in the team's record book, including highest all-time shooting percentage, fourth all-time in rebounds (3,671), third in blocks (700), third in free throws made (1,711), and ninth in points scored (6,127).

On June 22, 1987, the Chicago Bulls brought me back in a trade to provide backup for Dave Corzine — for whom I had been traded five years earlier. The Bulls also had a young player by the name of Michael Jordan, who you may have heard about. Michael was in his fourth season, averaging 35 points per game but still four years away from his first of six NBA championship rings. I was looking forward to contributing in the low post for Chicago. I felt that this was a team on the rise and would be a real contender. I felt that I had been a real contributor to Chicago during my first hitch, but now was an opportunity, even though I was no longer a young player, to help them reach and achieve a championship. Chicago fans were also energized. Michael's style created an excitement, whereas before basketball in Chicago was a bit conservative, and the only time people really came out was when Boston, Los Angeles, or Philadelphia came to town.

While it was true that I was not the dominant force I had been during earlier Bulls seasons — I was averaging 4.2 points and 2.6 rebounds in 15.5 minutes a game — I felt that I had knowledge as a veteran and specialized skills that would enable me to play a solid role on this growing team. But the team didn't share those feelings, and I was disappointed when on December 24, after only 24 games, the Bulls waived me.

I was pleased, however, when the Boston Celtics picked me up a couple weeks later to be a backup for Robert Parish and Brad Lohaus. I was the old man on the team with guys like Larry Bird, Kevin McHale, Dennis Johnson, and Danny Ainge.

So there I was, 21 years after seeing my first professional basketball game, back at Boston Garden, two days away from my last professional basketball game. Over the years many people have asked me questions about that last half season with the Celtics, assuming that it must have been a difficult time for me. I no longer was a star or even a starter, but believe me when I say it was a happy time.

First, a true professional loves the game. Because of the love for the game, the "great ones create." An integral part of creativity is flexibility and the willingness to adjust. If playing a few good minutes a game contributed to winning, I was glad to give it my best. My old nemesis Bill Walton was a big part of the Celtics' championship the year before in 1986, not because he scored or rebounded like he did as a young man but because he was a smart player who focused on what he could still do well. He also used his intelligence and generous personality to provide leadership both on the floor and in the locker room.

The Celtics, especially Larry Bird, welcomed me and gave me the same opportunities they had given to Walton. Larry went out of his way to assure me that I was not expected to do any more than I could — that I should play my game, help on defense, rebound on the weak side, and go for inside shots when the opportunities came. I welcomed this lack of pressure from a team that obviously adhered to the highest standards of excellence.

Larry Bird and I actually enjoyed a friendship that went back to my early days in the ABA. He and I had met at a basketball camp while he was at Indiana State. He was a nice young kid, and I shared my time with him. He appreciated and never forgot that and visited me occasionally while I played with the Kentucky Colonels. I was fond of Larry then and am proud to say he remains a friend of mine. As a player, it sounds silly to say that Larry was great. Everyone knows that. But few truly understand *how* great.

Second, the Celtics had a sense of balance that I had not felt since my days with the 1975 Colonels. At the heart of this were the "Big Three:" Bird, McHale, and Parish. They knew their roles and played them to perfection. It was a complementary relationship. Larry was the main focus on offense, taking the big shots and making the big plays. Kevin had those long arms and low-post moves. Robert was phenomenal in the paint — he could score if he had to, but his primary job was to rebound and run the court. It was a pleasure to be part of such a tight team. As an aside, I am one of only three people ever to play with *both* Michael Jordan and Larry Bird. The others are Danny Ainge and Sam Vincent.

Third, the Celtic legacy of greatness was evident within the Boston organization. They were truly professional. Many of the organizations today are very similar in how they treat the athlete, but that wasn't always the case. Back then, the Boston Celtics were long known for doing things first class; the same couldn't be said for many of the other franchises. That extended to the "small things" in life. For example, the Celtics made certain that the player's uniforms were always prepared. They made sure that they were clean and that they were laid out and ready for each game. Sounds simple, but everywhere else I'd been, it was the responsibility of the player to make sure that the uniforms were clean and ready for game day. This was a proud franchise, and it showed! The great Celtics' patriarch, Arnold "Red" Auerbach, was quick to make me feel at home in a Boston uniform and reminded me more than once of his motto: "Once a Celtic, always a Celtic," regardless of how many games a player actually played.

Fourth, although my role was very limited during my time with the Boston Celtics, I went deeper into the playoffs than at any other time in my previous 11 years in the NBA. Under the guidance of head coach K.C. Jones, we won the division title, finishing 57-25, and earning home-court advantage throughout the playoffs. We had a few things going against us, however. Bill Walton was recovering from his latest foot injury and would not play NBA ball again. Kevin McHale had missed the early part of the season also with a foot injury. The first round in the playoffs had been easy, a 3-to-1 romp over the New York Knicks. However, in our Eastern Conference Semifinals against Atlanta, our veterans, including Larry, Robert, and Danny, all had to play big minutes in what was a grinding, hard-fought effort. It all came down to the fourth quarter in Game 7 when Larry scored 20 points and we won 118-116. That's when age started to play against us. Our guys were exhausted from the struggle against Atlanta, and we were up next against the up-and-coming "Bad Boys": the Detroit Pistons. This was a heated rivalry, and we had no trouble getting psyched for the games. Sometimes, though, old legs don't get the message from an energized brain.

June 1, 1988, was the date for Game 5 against Isiah Thomas, Joe Dumars, Dennis Rodman, Adrian Dantley, Bill Laimbeer, Vinnie Johnson, John Salley,

Rick Mahorn, and James Edwards. Detroit was looking for revenge against the Celtics for having put the hurt on them the year before. Detroit was also out to prove that they could win in Boston after 21 straight defeats at the Boston Garden. Twice, Detroit had gone up in the series, and twice we had tied it. In none of the four games was the deciding score greater than eight points, and our victory on May 30 had been by a single point. For a while it looked like things were going well at home in Game 5. We led by as much as 16 points. But then, through a combination of very aggressive play and stubborn defense, Detroit turned things around and never looked back, beating us by six points. John Salley, who has since become a friend, has said that he has a permanent lump on his head given to him courtesy of one of my elbows. Just for the record: I hope I gave it to John during this particular game!

Two days later, we traveled to Detroit. Our backs were up against the wall, but we were the Celtics and had every intention of taking the series back home for Game 7. It was not to be. Detroit closed us out 95-90. The Pistons would go on to lose in the Finals in a heartbreaking Game 7 against the Los Angeles Lakers. As for me — at the age of 38, I had played my last game of NBA basketball.

Do I remember my last shot? Honestly, I don't. I hope I made it. Maybe I expected there to be more. When, after about a year, it became obvious that there wouldn't be any more NBA shots, I made a short comeback with Bologna Arimo of the Italian League, where I averaged 12.3 points and 11 rebounds and made the European All-Star Team. Living in northern Italy, I had a great time playing ball, eating great food, and making some money at the end of my career. The experience was educational for me and for my family, but after one season, we wanted to return home to the good ol' USA.

A new chapter of life had begun, and I could walk away from basketball as a player for good, satisfied with my body of work.

My contributions as an NBA player include:
- Career .599 field goal percentage --- second-highest in NBA history
- Four-time NBA field goal percentage champion (1981-84)
- .600 or better field goal percentage in six different seasons
- Six-time NBA All-Star (1978, 1979, 1981, 1982, 1983, 1986)
- Regular season averages: 17.1 points and 10.1 rebounds
- All-Defensive Second Team (1978)
- Chicago Bulls all-time leader in blocked shots (1,029)
- Chicago Bulls club record field-goal percentage (.587)

- Led Chicago Bulls in scoring, rebounding, field goal shooting, and blocked shots in three consecutive seasons and four overall (1976-78 and 1981)
- Led Chicago Bulls in field goal shooting and blocked shots in 1980

My contributions to the sport of basketball, combining ABA and NBA achievements, include:

- Fifth in career ABA/NBA field goal percentage (.582); second all-time in both the NBA (.599) and ABA (.557)
- Fourth-highest shot blocker in pro basketball (ABA/NBA) history (3,178)
- Fifth-highest rebounder in pro basketball (ABA/NBA) history (16,330)
- 26th of all-time pro basketball (ABA/NBA) scorers (24,941)
- One of only 30 players to score a total of 24,000 or more points (ABA and NBA combined)
- Leading left-handed scorer in professional basketball (ABA/NBA) history
- All-Star in 11 of 17 years as a pro
- 13th best all-time for pro (ABA/NBA) minutes played (47,134)
- Appeared in 670 consecutive ABA/NBA games
- Ranked in the top 10 in rebounding in 12 of 17 ABA/NBA seasons
- Ranked in the top 10 in blocked shots in 13 of 17 ABA/NBA seasons
- Ranked in the top 10 in field goal percentage in 15 of 17 ABA/NBA seasons
- Named to *The Sporting News'* Top 50 of the first 50 Years of the NBA
- Named to Athlon's Top 50 of the first 50 Years of the NBA
- Kentucky Sports Hall of Fame (inducted with entire Kentucky Colonels 1975 ABA championship team in 2005)
- Florida Sports Hall of Fame (1974)
- Listed in Alex Sachare's 1997 book: *The Naismith Memorial Basketball Hall of Fame's 100 Greatest Basketball Players of All-Time*

So, what does it all mean beyond the numbers? As a man at the point in his life where looking back is starting to take on larger meaning, the individual statistics, though a source of personal pride, have grown less important than what basketball has provided me as a whole.

I was able to leave my childhood poverty from Chipley and help bring financial security and well-being to my parents — a wish in life that motivated me throughout my playing career and influenced every major decision I made.

I truly don't spend any time thinking about my legacy as a basketball player because my body of work speaks for itself. I'm not a household name, and I'm perfectly happy with that, knowing I earned the respect of my peers. Had I played entirely in the NBA or if the Kentucky Colonels still existed today, I'm sure I'd be remembered differently. But I chose to play in the ABA to better take care of my family and myself, and I'll always be happy with that.

I was able, with my wife Enola Gay, to build a great family of my own in Jacksonville, Florida. After my playing days were over, I chose to return back to my roots in Jacksonville. After my success at Jacksonville University, I received a key to the city, and I knew that's where I wanted to be when I retired. I'm not the only one in the family who didn't want to drift far from Chipley; my sister Ossie spent more than three decades working in Houston in public education, and after she retired, she moved back to Chipley. There's not a whole lot there, but if you're looking for peace and quiet, that's the one thing you'll find.

Enola and I have been together since junior college. In case you're wondering, her rather interesting name comes from the name of the plane that dropped the atomic bomb on Hiroshima. While pregnant with Enola, her mother had seen a movie about that event and the name stuck. We count ourselves blessed to have five fantastic children — Shawna, Priya, Tifany, O.J. (Otis James), and Artis II — as well as three grandchildren. For those of you interested in basketball trivia, Priya, who played basketball for Louisiana Tech, and I are the only father-daughter combination to both have played in an NCAA basketball final. My other children were never too interested in pursuing basketball, and I consciously chose to never push it on them. We've worked hard to give our kids a quality education and a fulfilling life.

In other professional ventures, I feel privileged and proud to have maintained an ongoing and positive relationship with Jacksonville University where I have been involved in many promotional activities. I have also worked with a mechanical engineering company, W.W. Gay Mechanical Contractor, Inc., in the area of private development and have played a part in turning the company into the largest mechanical contractor in the Southeast. It is very satisfying work, though completely different from basketball.

Charitable work, NBA promotions, and golf take up the rest of my spare time. And, yes, I still run the court whenever I get the chance. The hamstrings tend to hurt a bit more. The vertical leap may not be what it once was. But the fire is still there when the game gets going.

Now, when I play basketball or think about the days gone by, I focus less for some reason on what I did and more on the people I grew to know and respect. Their opinions, more than the statistics, have become of greater and greater importance to me.

My teammate from the Chicago Bulls, Norm Van Lier, once told a reporter that if he had a son, he'd want him to be just like Artis Gilmore. I'd give back a ton of marks in the record book in exchange for such a generous, thoughtful comment. (Thankfully, I don't have to!) Thank you, Norm.

My friend Lloyd "Pinky" Gardner, trainer for the Kentucky Colonels, repeatedly bragged that I never complained about pain. I didn't — not for any macho reason — just because I loved to play and never wanted to miss a game.

Former Indiana Pacers forward Darnell Hillman was a guy I battled game after game. He was a great leaper, and we always tried to outdo each other in shot blocking. The real prize was being able to block the dunk of the other guy. I'll always value the fact that Darnell thought enough of our competitiveness to say: "He was my greatest — a lot of players' greatest — rival."

Hall-of-Famer Bob McAdoo has said that I had enough strength to "flatten the Spalding" on you. There are worse ways to be remembered.

So, how exactly *would* I choose to be remembered, if not for my on-court accomplishments? Someone somewhere sometime described me in an article as "Tough, Durable, and Consistent."

Okay, that may or may not sound very flashy to you, but I think it rings pretty true. I never elbowed my way through crowds to reach the limelight. I only elbowed my way to the basket to do my job. In doing so, more than one sports writer described me as "methodical." To this I will answer, not in my own words, but as with so many other times in many other places, the words of my mentor and coach, Hubie Brown, who replied, "Yes, Artis was methodical. But you could hit him with an ax and he would still take you to the rim. He was as strong as anybody."

The chapter of my life titled 'Professional Basketball Player' was a page-turning action thriller that no player really wants to put down — but we all have our limits. The lessons I learned, the people I met, and the experiences I endured through the game of basketball undoubtedly shaped the other chapters in my life, which shows how my passion for basketball transcended the game itself and continues to do so to this day.

"Tough, Durable, and Consistent." Yeah, I can live with that.

Career Statistics

Teams

Gardner-Webb (junior college, 1967-69)

Jacksonville University (college, 1969-71)

Kentucky Colonels (ABA, 1971-76)

Chicago Bulls (NBA, 1976-82)

San Antonio Spurs (NBA, 1982-87)

Chicago Bulls (NBA, 1987)

Boston Celtics (NBA, 1988)

Arimo Bologna (Italy, 1988-89)

NBA + ABA

Games played: 1329

Points Per Game: 18.8

Rebounds Per Game: 12.3

Assists Per Game: 2.3

Blocks Per Game: 2.4

Steals Per Game: 0.6

FG%: .582

ABA

Games played: 420

Points Per Game: 22.3

Rebounds Per Game: 17.1

Assists Per Game: 3.0

Blocks Per Game: 3.4

Steals Per Game: 0.7

FG%: .557

NBA

Games played: 909
Points Per Game: 17.1
Rebounds Per Game: 10.1
Assists Per Game: 2.0
Blocks Per Game: 1.9
Steals Per Game: 0.5
FG%: .599

NCAA (Jacksonville University)

Games played: 54
Points Per Game: 24.3
Rebounds Per Game: 22.7
Assists Per Game: 1.7
FG%: .574

SOURCES

- http://20secondtimeout.blogspot.com/2009/02/abas-unsung-heroes.html
- http://articles.chicagotribune.com/2006-04-23/sports/0604230266_1_playoff-norm-van-lier-entire-series
- http://articles.latimes.com/2010/mar/14/sports/la-sp-crowe-20100311
- http://articles.sun-sentinel.com/1991-06-23/news/9103050340_1_burrows-dolphins-jacksonville-university
- https://www.basketball-reference.com/players/g/gilmoar01.html
- https://www.basketball-reference.com/teams/CHI/leaders_career.html
- http://www.bbc.com/sport/boxing/16146367
- http://www.celtic-nation.com/interviews/artis_gilmore/artis_gilmore_page3.htm
- http://www.chipleypaper.com/article/20151009/NEWS/151009163
- http://www.espn.com/tvlistings/show33transcript.html
- http://www.espn.com/nba/halloffame11/story/_/page/110811-Gilmore/artis-gilmore-entering-hall-fame
- https://www.forbes.com/sites/monteburke/2014/01/07/the-nba-finally-puts-an-end-to-the-greatest-sports-deal-of-all-time/#71da49754f0b
- http://grantland.com/features/how-jacksonville-earned-credit-card-paul-hemphill/
- http://history.bulls.com/1970s-and-the-chicago-bulls/
- http://www.hoophall.com/hall-of-famers/artis-gilmore/
- http://www.jacksonville.com/article/20100212/SPORTS/801257400
- http://judolphins.com/information/hall_of_fame/gilmore_artis?view=bio
- http://judolphins.com/sports/mbkb/2016-17_Mens_Basketball_Record_Book.pdf

- http://www.nba.com/history/players/gilmore_bio.html
- http://www.nba.com/history/players/reed_bio.html
- http://www.nba.com/history/players/thomas_bio.html
- https://www.newspapers.com/newspage/73471394/
- https://www.newspapers.com/newspage/7833129/
- https://www.newspapers.com/newspage/180169206/
- http://www.nytimes.com/2004/03/14/sports/inside-the-nba-grizzlies-10-man-rotation-spins-success.html?_r=0
- http://people.com/archive/chicagos-artis-gilmore-is-4-5-million-worth-of-center-that-is-and-isnt-a-lot-of-bull-vol-11-no-8/
- http://www.remembertheaba.com/FanMemories/DallasFanMemories.html
- http://www.remembertheaba.com/onlyintheabamaterial/onlyintheaba4.html
- http://www.remembertheaba.com/onlyintheabamaterial/onlyintheaba/WrestlingBear/WrestlingBear.html
- http://www.remembertheaba.com/ABAArticles/PattisonArticleGilmore.html
- http://www.remembertheaba.com/tributematerial/lucas.html
- http://retirechicagobullsjersey53.blogspot.com/
- https://www.si.com/vault/2009/02/09/105777161/the-fly-who-came-in-from-the-cold
- https://www.si.com/vault/2004/11/15/8191994/getting-by-on-146-mil
- https://www.si.com/vault/1986/04/07/643897/a-crashing-success
- https://www.sports-reference.com/cbb/players/artis-gilmore-1.html
- https://www.sports-reference.com/cbb/schools/jacksonville/1970.html
- https://sports.yahoo.com/cleveland-cavaliers-scouted-1970-expansion-draft-trading-cards-224426478.html?y20=1
- http://www.washingtonpost.com/wp-srv/sports/longterm/memories/1996/nba/iverson.htm
- http://wavemagazineonline.com/dolphins-say-farewell-to-ju-basketball-legend-ernie-fleming/
- Bird, Larry, and Bob Ryan. *Drive: the story of my life.* Bantam Books, 199
- Levitt, Zak, director. Bad Boys. ESPN *30 for 30*, 17 Apr. 2014.
- Pluto, Terry. *Loose balls: the short, wild life of the American Basketball Association.* Simon & Schuster Paperbacks, 2007.

About the Authors

Artis Gilmore

Artis Gilmore is a legendary Hall of Fame basketball player and one of only a small handful of basketball greats to have demonstrated persistent dominance in both the American Basketball Association and the National Basketball Association. He is widely regarded as one of the most talented and skilled big men in the history of the game. Artis was enshrined in the Naismith Memorial Basketball Hall of Fame in 2011.

Mark Bruner

Mark Bruner is the 30-year owner of J4 Communications, a sales and marketing communications agency. He continues to play amateur basketball after 61 years of trying. He helped establish Still Here Basketball, Inc., a non-profit charitable organization, dedicated in part to helping young basketball players in financial need.

REID GRIFFITH FONTAINE

Reid Griffith Fontaine is a clinical psychologist, criminal lawyer, and forensic research consultant. He has held scientist and professor appointments at Duke University, University of Arizona, University of Rome and Florida State University, and has published more than 35 peer-reviewed articles in interdisciplinary law and behavioral science. His first book, *The Mind of the Criminal,* was published in 2012 by Cambridge University Press. He currently holds a Visiting Research Fellow appointment at Duke University.

Index

Issel, Dan 12, 48, 50, 53, 55, 57, 59, 72, 125, 132, 135, 136, 142
Iverson, Allen 12, 25, 141

J

Jabali, Warren 48
Jackson, Phil 74, 139
Jacksonville Coliseum 70
Jacksonville Dolphins 30, 65, 69, 70, 73, 75
Jacksonville University 12, 30, 32, 38, 39, 65, 70, 73, 160, 162, 163
James, LeBron 12
Johnson, Chris 101
Johnson, Dennis 156
Johnson, Gus 49
Johnson, Magic 20, 154
Johnson, Marques 101
Johnson, Mickey 63, 150
Johnson, Neil 45
Johnson, Vinnie 157
Jones, Bobby 40
Jones, Caldwell 132, 142
Jones, Collis 50
Jones, K.C. 22, 157
Jones, Sam 21
Jones, Wali 31
Jones, Wil 53, 135, 136, 143
Jones, Wilbert 58, 59
Jordan, DeAndre 12
Jordan, Michael 12, 79, 80, 139, 155, 157
Joyce, Kevin 58, 59, 60

K

Kamla, Rick 125
Keller, Billy 59, 136
Kenon, Larry 50, 53, 96
Kentucky Athletic Hall of Fame 126
Kentucky Colonels 12, 41, 44, 46, 50, 55, 56, 57, 58, 59, 65, 72, 77, 78, 87, 89, 91, 129, 131, 132, 133, 138, 139, 142, 143, 144, 162

Kentucky Wildcats 71, 132
Kinne, Fran 8
Knight, Billy 59, 108, 130, 132
Knight, Bobby 88
Kovler, Jon 63
Kraft, Jack 31
Kropp, Tom 63
Kruer, Curtis 66

L

Ladner, Wendell 50, 130
Laimbeer, Bill 25, 157
Lanier, Bob 72, 88
Laskowski, John 63
Leonard, Slick 132
Littles, Gene 135, 136
Lohaus, Brad 156
Los Angeles Lakers 12, 20, 151, 154, 158
Los Angeles Stars 131
Loughery, Levin 132
Love, Bob 150
Lucas, Jerry 21
Lucas, Maurice 52, 55, 58, 75, 90, 142, 143, 151
Lue, Tyronn 12

M

Macy, Kyle 101
Madden, Jack 50, 55
Maddox, James 113
Mahorn, Rick 158
Malone, Moses 13, 127, 132, 154
Maloy, Mike 66
Maravich, Pete 76
Marin, Jack 63
May, Scott 63, 150
McAdoo, Bob 99, 101, 155, 161
McCarthy, Babe 61, 135
McClain, Ted 53, 55, 59, 135, 136, 142
McDaniels, Jim 31, 48, 58, 71
McGinnis, George 47, 59, 60, 61, 93, 135, 137
McHale, Kevin 156, 157

Selke, Ken 66
Simon, Walt 45, 50
Simpson, Ralph 49
Sloan, Jerry 149, 151
Sojourner, Willie 45, 50
Spirits of St. Louis 52, 136, 142
Sprewell, Latrell 26
Starr, Keith 63
St. Bonaventure University 72
Storen, Mike 40
Swisher Gym 70

T

The Traveling Daedals 101
Thomas, Isiah 25, 157
Thomas, Ron 50, 56, 58, 59, 135,
    136, 143
Thompson, David 13, 95, 117, 132
Thompson, George 48
Thorn, Rod 153
Tomjanovich, Rudy 94
Tormohlen, Gene 63, 151
Tresvant, John 44
Twardzik, Dave 151

U

UCLA Bruins 73, 75
Unseld, Wes 44
Utah Stars 133

V

Vallely, John 76
Vanak, John 53, 59, 60

van Breda Kolff, Jan 58, 143
Vance, David 58
Vance, Van 45
Van Lier, Norm 150, 161
Vincent, Sam 157
Virginia Squires 45, 134, 135, 143

W

Walker, Chet 31
Wallace, Ben 82
Walton, Bill 81, 151, 152, 156, 157
Wasdin, Tom 8, 65, 66
Washington, Kermit 94
Wedeking, Vaughn 66, 68, 71, 72
Western Kentucky Hilltoppers 71
Westhead, Paul 101
West, Jerry 20
Whatley, Ennis 101
White, Arthur 69
White, Jo Jo 25
Wicks, Sidney 76, 87
Williams, Chuck 50, 54, 55
Williams, James 130
Williams, Joe 8, 65, 68, 70
Williamson, John 50
Winter, Tex 139
Wirtz, Arthur 63
Wooden, John 75, 76, 77, 87

MORE SPORTS BOOKS
PUBLISHED BY ACCLAIM PRESS

Kentucky Colonels of the American Basketball Association

An inside look at one of the most intriguing times in the history of professional basketball; and the city of Louisville and the state of Kentucky were enjoying every bit of it.

And then as quickly as the Colonels appeared, they were gone. They had been around just long enough to win a world championship and showcase not only some of the best basketball players in the history of the game, but also some of its most colorful characters.

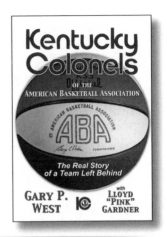

Kentucky Colonels: Shots from the Sidelines

Turn back the clock four decades with this visual masterpiece featuring over 400 photos from official sideline photographer Mark Gordon and captions by Colonel trainer Lloyd "Pink" Gardner.

Through these images, fans of the American Basketball Association will remember the high flying, intense action of that rough and tumble league, including stars like Louie Dampier, Artis Gilmore and Dan Issel from the Colonels, and other well-known greats such as "Dr. J" Julius Erving, Wes Unseld, and George Gervin, among others.

The sequel to the 2011 best seller, *Kentucky Colonels: The Real Story of a Team Left Behind*, ...*Shots from the Sidelines* brings back the sights from every season from 1970-76...from the shots, the blocks, the drives, the slam dunks, the locker room, and even a few fights...all are captured in these vivid photographs from Mark Gordon.

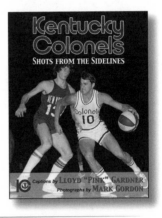

Barnstorming America

In an era when women had only recently been given the right to vote and the Great Depression made jobs of any kind hard to come by, American women of the 1930s faced an uphill battle when it came to accessing opportunities to work outside the home. About the same time, basketball was gaining popularity in America and its schools. Girls were allowed to play basketball, although the rules were modified to accommodate the "weaker sex". Many girls excelled at basketball to the extent that they wanted to keep playing after high school. But apart from Amateur Athletic Union programs and the rare college teams, organized basketball after high school was out of reach of most women.

In 1936, C.M. "Ole" Olson recruited the best female basketball players he could find and formed the All American Red Heads — the very first women's professional basketball team to hit America's roads and operate successfully. This is the story of the women who helped reshape America's attitudes toward women in sports and paved the way for today's professional women's leagues.

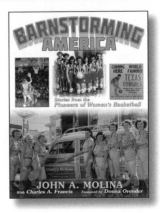

The Boys From Corbin: America's Greatest Little Sports Town

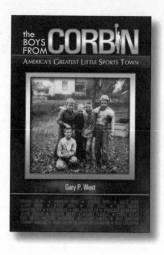

What do the Los Angeles Lakers, St. Louis Cardinals, New York Knicks, San Diego Chargers, Oakland Raiders, Kentucky Wildcats, Louisville Cardinals, Western Kentucky Hilltoppers, Furman Paladins and the Eastern Kentucky Colonels all have in common? They have had all had star athletes who began their careers as Corbin Redhounds.

For four decades, the 30's, 40's, 50's, and 60's, Corbin High School sports were the glue that held the town together. For those who worked on the railroad, cut or hauled timber, or chiseled and drug coal from the nearby mines, football and basketball were a diversion from the daily chore or providing for their families. Sports were the common denominator that transcended the economic levels of Corbin's citizenry.

The Boys from Corbin—America's Greatest Little Sports Town is not just a story… it's a phenomenon.

Better Than Gold: Olympian Kenny Davis and the Most Controversial Basketball Game in History

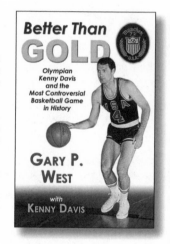

An Olympics like no other… Every four years, the whole world turns its eyes upon a single gathering of the planet's best athletes for a series of sporting events. In the summer of 1972, however, there occurred such an Olympic gathering much unlike any other before it or, thankfully, since.

An unprecedented terrorist attack had invaded the tranquility of Olympic Village, leaving 11 Israeli athletes dead and the world aghast. As the USA's team took the court, there was an unnerving tension building as they prepared to play against the best and most experienced Soviet Union team ever assembled.

This is the story of Kenny Davis, captain of that very team, a sharp-shooting farm boy from Kentucky, cast onto the world's center stage in the challenge of a lifetime. Discover what Davis and all of the members of his 1972 USA Olympic Basketball Team did in amidst tragedy and injustice; something much more valuable than just winning a ball game, something much Better Than Gold.

Legacies of Kentucky Mountain Basketball: Champions and Palaces of the Mid-1950s

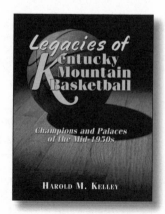

A look back at what once was the heart and soul of sports in the beautiful, but rugged mountains of Kentucky is what *Legacies of Kentucky Mountain Basketball* does with photographs from today.

Legacies of Kentucky Mountain Basketball … is about the golden era of high school basketball in Kentucky, high school basketball that was as close to the original game as we will ever see again.

This book features the towns and high schools of the 13th, 14th and 15th Regions of the Commonwealth, including detailed accounts of the 1953-54, 1954-55, and 1955-56 seasons.

Kentucky High School Basketball Encyclopedia

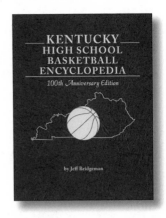

After years of painstaking research and in cooperation with the Kentucky Association of Basketball Coaches and the Kentucky High School Athletics Association, we are pleased to announce the expanded edition of the Kentucky High School Basketball Encyclopedia, by statistician and editor Jeff Bridgeman.

The *Kentucky High School Basketball Encyclopedia, 100th Anniversary Edition* has it all…every team, every school, every year from the beginning of high school basketball in Kentucky—boys and girls—through 2017!

NO sports library or reference section will be complete without it. Reserve your copy today!

King Kelly Coleman: Kentucky's Greatest Basketball Legend

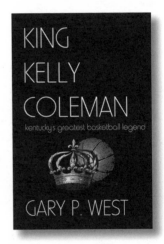

In a state where the love of basketball itself is legendary, there are its rare heroes who also, through the dispassionate lens of history, rise to legendary status. When that legend rises so far above the others as to acquire mythical or rather, folk hero, proportions – and then enigmatically vanishes- you have King Kelly Coleman.

This shy, humble mountain boy blessed with extraordinary talent and drive captured Kentucky's hearts and its all-time record books with performances that have yet to be equaled – even half a century later. Never before in print, the authorized King Kelly Coleman story, is told by award-winning author Gary P. West, from actual interviews and information from Coleman himself.

Sinister Influences: Kentucky's Fabulous Five and the Point-Shaving Scandal of 1951

The passion that is University of Kentucky basketball's Big Blue Nation is not a recent phenomenon. In fact, fans' maniacal devotion to the 'Cats traces back to Coach Adolph Rupp's early days at UK in the 1930's. As Rupp grew into his job, his teams steadily grew more formidable until they became nearly invincible in what came to be known as UK's "glory years," 1946-1951. In that time frame, Kentucky's Fabulous Five merely: won the National Invitational Tournament (NIT) once; finished runner-up once; won the National Collegiate Athletic Association (NCAA) Tournament three times and could have won it a fourth time and formed the nucleus of the United States Olympic team which won the Gold Medal.

Then, one October day in 1951, the roof caved in. Authorities arrested the stars, Ralph Beard and Alex Groza, on charges of conspiring with gamblers to "shave points" as the "fixers'" felt that UK's teams were talented enough to win by any chosen margin. While that activity was poor ethics anywhere, it was illegal in the State of New York. As many of Kentucky's games were played in Madison Square Garden — "The Mecca of College Basketball" — the players were guilty of a serious crime. [o]Although UK was the highest profile team involved, the point shaving scandal was not limited to them. Before it was over, 30 players from seven schools were implicated.

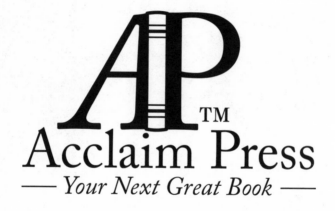